TEACHING ENGLISH
in the
KEY STAGE 3
LITERACY
STRATEGY

Geoff Dean

David Fulton Publishers
London

Reading maketh a full man;
conference a ready man;
and writing an exact man.

Essays 50 – Of Studies
Francis Bacon 1561–1626

Dedicated to my colleagues and friends of the
National Association of Advisers in English (NAAE)
from whom I have learned so much.

David Fulton Publishers Ltd
Ormond House, 26–27 Boswell Street, London WC1N 3JZ

www.fultonpublishers.co.uk

First published in Great Britain in 2002 by David Fulton Publishers

Note: The right of Geoff Dean to be identified as the author of this work has been
asserted by him in accordance with the Copyright, Designs and Patents Act 1988.

© Geoff Dean 2002

British Library Cataloguing in Publication Data
A catalogue record for this book is available from the British Library.

ISBN 1 85346 860 6

Typeset by Textype Typesetters, Cambridge
Printed and bound in Great Britain by Bell and Bain Ltd, Glasgow

Contents

Preface

It is not my intention to argue a case for or against the introduction of a National Literacy Strategy (NLS) at Key Stage 3. In actual fact, there is not a single '*Literacy Strategy*', as such; there is a Key Stage 3 National Strategy, comprising a number of 'strands'. The *English strand* and the *literacy strand* are linked, but are still only two of a number of components of this broadly based programme intended to positively change the educational attainment of pupils in Years 7 to 9 of their secondary education in English schools, from September 2001.

The Key Stage 3 English and literacy programmes are a fact. They are not statutory, but in our current educational climate their implementation is expected in all secondary schools. If the Department for Education and Skills (DfES) requires the programme to be undertaken; if it provides money for training through Standards Funds; if it causes hundreds of Key Stage 3 Literacy Consultants to be appointed; if it links the programmes with 'targets' at LEA and school levels; evaluates the programme through OFSTED and LEA inspectorates, we can all be assured that this is an initiative not to be ignored.

The words 'practical guide' in the title require a short explanation. This is *not* a 'tips for teachers' book. It does contain at different points some models of planning, and a few suggestions of lesson approaches for classroom use, as examples of the general principles being promoted by the NLS. But it is not one of the myriad books currently being hurriedly churned out by the publishing trade offering ready-made lesson content. The many flyers accumulating in Heads of English departments' in-trays speak for themselves. 'Practical' means 'of or concerned with practice'. At this, possibly, unique watershed time in the history of teaching English, all those engaged in its day-to-day deliberations, teaching and development should be embracing the opportunity to rethink the possibilities of the subject currently available. 'Practical' in this context is about raising a number of the central issues to do with English, literacy and language learning in an attempt to cohere them more purposely for the benefit of English staff and all their other colleagues.

Many English departments will not need a book such as this one. English is taught with great skill and commitment in thousands of secondary schools; it is regularly 'vital, rigorous and effective, with an appropriate blend of the formal and creative' (*TES* 25 May 2001), as one critic of the Key Stage 3 Strategy claimed. Hundreds of thousands of pupils enjoy the subject and a large proportion of them achieve good results in English and English literature at GCSE. Larger numbers nationally attain more A–C passes than in any other subject.

Yet there are also many schools where English departments do not have the luxury of a full team of specialist subject staff to teach all classes. Where problems of recruitment have been most profound, there is often an assumption that 'anybody can teach English!', and RE teachers, historians, and others, have been drafted in, often to teach Year 7 and 8 classes, guided by programmes put together by bona fide English staff. There have been training problems, too. The Government made funds available to free some members of the English teams from each secondary school to attend two days of central LEA training, and to enable feedback and sharing of what had been learned with their colleagues in school. But the time made available was never sufficient, and the implications of some of the issues emerging from the training have simply not been fully addressed because of other, more demanding pressures.

Organisationally, English departments across the country offer a very mixed picture, despite the demands of monitoring agencies, such as OFSTED. At the end of a recent English Key Stage 3 training session I led, teachers from two secondary schools quietly approached me to confide that the departments in which they work currently do not have published, or even understood, schemes of work for Key Stage 3 classes. Eleven years after the introduction of the National Curriculum, the English teachers in those schools 'do their own thing' with pupils in Years 7, 8 and 9. I often undertake training in different parts of the country and know that these schools are by no means exceptional. English departments occupy a wide variety of places along a developmental continuum.

It is not unusual to hear complaints from parents reporting on behalf of their own children, and also from primary teachers speaking for those children they have previously taught, about Year 7 English lessons lacking the degree of challenge those youngsters would have experienced in their primary schools. Issues of continuity have often been neglected at the interface of Key Stages 2 and 3, with pupils' previous learning neither recognised nor accommodated in their new English curriculum. I still visit secondary schools where the textual resources for Key Stage 3 English lessons are undemanding and the department has neither a published view of teaching reading, nor a collaborative sense of what progression in reading might mean. Indeed, most teachers of English readily agree that they have never been trained to teach reading, and yet, enormous amounts of reading take place in English lessons.

Where Schemes of Work do guide the teaching arrangements of an English department, they do not always identify and articulate the actual specific or broad intended learning outcomes the pupils are expected to take from programmes of lessons. Even in those schools where the English department is able to demonstrate its own first-class provision and practices, that situation will not necessarily bring about a shared view of language and literacy development across the other subjects of the curriculum. Few secondary English teachers have ever been taught how to teach spelling, for instance, so there is little likelihood that other members of staff, teaching other subjects, have had that training either.

These factors in isolation, of course, would not justify introducing a major new initiative in a National Curriculum core subject, but, regarded together, they begin to make a more convincing case for necessary change. My own individual experiences and observations, as a local authority English Adviser and former OFSTED Inspector, would hardly represent an overwhelming body of evidence. Yet, when I regularly share such experiences and observations with many colleagues working in the same capacity in other LEAs, representing the whole possible range of schools and communities, they begin to take on real significance. Many of us agree about the sorts of improvements that need to be made, and a number of those are contained within the English strand.

So, while there are undoubtedly huge numbers of successful, even excellent, English departments, there are also certainly sufficient numbers of departments not yet paying rigorous attention to the details of their teaching programmes, particularly details of language *learning*. These departments make the necessity of a Key Stage 3 Strategy essential. And even the successful departments can be improved further by the thoughtful adoption of particular features of such an important, national shared enterprise. Successful departments are rarely successful at everything. Only the most stubbornly arrogant department would claim that it could not benefit from some sort of change, made after careful review.

I will declare an interest from the start: I believe that the Key Stage 3 English and literacy strands offer a positive opportunity for those concerned with the teaching of English to reposition themselves in a more consistent and coherent manner. The future direction of the subject has been less and less clear since 1990, and some sort of significant, potentially transforming occurrence has to allow those connected with its practice to rethink new possibilities. The link with literacy development is also to be welcomed, and English teachers should be pleased about and keen to exploit this rare period when the spotlight has been placed on matters of language and learning as a national priority. For the first time ever there is a unique opportunity for English departments to reposition and relate themselves within the range of language responsibilities shared with their colleagues in other subjects, and backed with government support. In the main, the Strategy is a 'good thing', although there are a number of unanswered questions relating to it, requiring careful examination. Some of those will be raised in the ensuing chapters.

I have come to these conclusions partly because I have been assured by the nature and attitudes of those who have put the Key Stage 3 programme together. The NLS secondary team care for the subject and its development. While it has been a government sponsored initiative, the mistakes of the early nineties – calling on politically motivated amateur enthusiasts and zealots to supervise the writing of English-related documentation – have not been repeated. This book will, therefore, reflect a broadly approving stance, with a few sceptical enquiries.

The English strand of the Key Stage 3 Strategy has been designed to

- provide a clearer entitlement curriculum for pupils in English across Key Stage 3;
- help track more firmly progression in English across the Key Stage;
- make the study of language as the conveyor of meaning more important;
- give greater attention to learning through language and literacy engagements;
- pay increased attention to word level, sentence level and text level considerations, and use them as more secure foundations of language learning;
- continue the sorts of learning to which pupils have become accustomed in Key Stages 1 and 2 into the secondary school; and
- 'make the transparent more apparent', that is to make clearer and much more obvious to pupils and teachers the sorts of practices and events currently familiar in English classrooms, but not always framed and foregrounded as learning activities, to which closer attention has to be paid.

Of course, the business of improving the language and literacy skills of young people is not just a matter of concern for schools, and certainly not solely for the teachers of English. Other equally important developments need immediate attention if real and sustained growth is to be achieved. The tests administered to pupils at the end of Key Stage 3 require serious review and overhaul. Every English teacher in the country could quickly reel off a whole set of reasons to demonstrate how inadequate the current test is as a piece of assessment apparatus. Fourteen-year-old pupils have to show they can answer comprehension questions on a passage of Shakespeare. They also answer comprehension questions on another piece of text, and write an essay (possibly a story, possibly in another type of text). Optional test materials recently devised for pupils at the end of Years 7 and 8 have begun to explore different and broader ways of seeking to discover how pupils can engage with and respond to a variety of texts, and show that they can recognise the way language functions in them. The Government, through its assessment agency, the Qualifications and Curriculum Authority (QCA), has to find the courage to remove the Shakespeare element from this particular test situation and shift it to the context of teacher assessment. Nobody wants to see its total removal from the Key Stage 3 programme; just a readjustment in relation to its status. Successive Secretaries of State have so far been reluctant to face this problem, as they fear offending the readership of newspapers such as the *Daily Mail*, with its inevitable charges of 'lowering of standards' and (an unconscious ironical cliché) 'dumbing down' if such a radical move was to be made! Until, however, the tests at the end of Key Stage 2, the end of Years 7 and 8, and at the end of Key Stage 3 have obvious consistency and demonstrate progression on common grounds, they cannot be taken very seriously.

Other, associated, developments could also make considerable positive differences to the improvement of language and literacy development nationally. Pinning all our hopes on three to five hours a week of focused study in schools is an extremely optimistic enterprise. A huge proportion of the population would benefit from toddler-based literacy programmes that began with the first visit of the health visitor. Literacy remains a female province in much of our culture; many males feel unable or disinclined to offer role modelling of reading and writing practices to their children. Too many children in our society arrive at school with undeveloped literacy skills, unfamiliar with reading and unused to the mark-making activities likely to lead to early writing. Libraries remain underfunded and lack real influence; schools, with their technological resources, are only just beginning to learn how they can offer real facilities to improve literacy more generally in their wider communities. The influence of popular culture and the everyday distractions, particularly of moving images, tempting children away from the sorts of literacy approved and promoted in schools, are legion. School-based literacy procedures face huge pressures. Little discussion has actually taken place about whether the 'common sense' notion of 'literacy', as represented in the current materials, is the one that deserves greatest attention. Yet, while the outcomes of our educational system are measured through the production of written texts by young people, we have to continue to ensure that they manage that process as well as they can.

Finally, it has to be repeated that the Strategy, like its equivalents in Key Stages 1 and 2, is not statutory. No law requires its adoption in every English secondary school. Yet, OFSTED has been alerted to seek literacy as a cross-curricular development, and its inspectors will be looking for a more active, engaging programme of English teaching, based on the recommendations of the 'four part lesson'. Most English departments will have to make at least some minor adjustments to ensure that they integrate fully the previous literacy/English experiences of their new intake of 11-year-olds. In these circumstances most English teachers have recognised that 'no change is *not* an option', as Alastair West, an English Subject Officer at QCA, stated in a public meeting.

Therefore, an English department already guided by Schemes of Work based on well-defined learning objectives; accustomed to moving its incoming pupils on from the point of learning achieved in their primary schools; regularly teaching active, engaging lessons confidently devised to improve pupils as readers, writers, speakers and listeners constructed on solid word level, sentence level and text level structures would need make no further changes to its arrangements! Departments not quite managing to integrate all these features at this time will probably want to make the appropriate adjustments.

Geoff Dean
Milton Keynes
January 2002

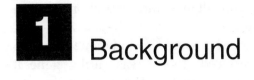

1 Background

In September 1998 the UK government introduced the National Literacy Strategy to primary schools in England. While in opposition, the Labour Party had made clear its intention to improve the literacy skills of primary pupils, and the future Prime Minister, Tony Blair, committed himself to his 'three priorities: Education, Education and Education!' In February 1997 David Blunkett, then Shadow Secretary of State for Education, published a preliminary consultation report compiled by a specially commissioned Literacy Task Force. Even at that stage it was clear that the Task Force intended to adopt and expand the model of the National Literacy Project, introduced two years earlier into 13, mostly inner city, pilot Local Education Authorities (LEAs) by John Major's Conservative government. That summer, following the Labour general election victory in May 1997, Mr Blunkett – then fully installed as Secretary of State – published a final report, setting out details for a 'steady consistent Strategy' (DfEE 1997). This Strategy, dedicated to 'raising standards of literacy' as a central aim for the whole education service, was intended for introduction to all primary schools from September 1998.

The new programme was underpinned by an ambitious national target of 80 per cent of 11-year-old pupils reaching Level 4, the standard expected for their age range in the National Curriculum tests in English, to be administered in 2002. This was ambitious in two ways. First, it is worth remembering that when the National Curriculum was introduced in 1989, Level 4 was regarded as the median point of the age group. About half of all 11-year-old pupils were then thought capable of achieving such a result. By an enormous sleight of hand, during the next decade, successive governments managed to convince themselves – and the press – that Level 4 (never an objective set of criteria in relation to English learning in the first place) was within the grasp of a far greater proportion of the age group. Secondly, as the actual proportion reaching this standard was 57 per cent in the 1996 tests, it is possible to understand the considerable scepticism about how realistic such a target appeared when first mooted.

Even more noteworthy, at the time, was the Government's expectation of the adoption of the Strategy by all primary schools, without the assistance of statutory pressure. The Literacy Strategy has never been a legal requirement; its establishment depending on one early paragraph in the August report:

> The approach to teaching literacy should be based on the NLP and should be adopted in every primary school, *unless a school can demonstrate through its literacy action plan, schemes of work and performance in Key Stage 2 tests, that the approach it has adopted is at least as effective.*
>
> (DfEE 1997, emphasis added)

For those of us concerned with LEA advisory, consultancy and inspection work in that period those words were enormously powerful.

However hard many individual primary teachers were working in their own classrooms, before the Strategy was introduced there was little general understanding about how pupils learned language and made progress in and through literacy. While the teaching of initial reading was undertaken, often very successfully, in Key Stage 1, teachers of junior school pupils failed to build sufficiently strongly on those early stages. Much of the literacy/language curriculum in the primary years was based in narrative fiction, with only minimal attention paid to non-fiction and the sort of information-based textual material regularly employed in secondary schools. Primary pupils practised enormous quantities of writing, but few teachers had sufficient knowledge of the ways in which their pupils might possibly continue to develop as writers to bring about genuine progression. In those instances where a few schools had devised 'action plans' for literacy, they rarely articulated or outlined pupils' language and literacy learning opportunities.

Suddenly, during the spring and summer months of 1998, primary teachers were faced with a formidable and intimidating training programme, challenging all their former practices and beliefs. Most frighteningly, according to huge numbers of teachers, was the expectation that every primary teacher should plan and teach a Literacy Hour every day. This 'prescriptive strait- jacket', as it was frequently represented in the educational press and school staffrooms, was a recommended model of teaching to be carried out in all primary classes every day. This hour was expected to begin with 15 minutes of whole-class textual study with the teacher didactically demonstrating approaches to reading or writing; it was then to continue with 15 minutes of word or sentence study (phonics, vocabulary or grammar), followed by 20 minutes of independent pupil practice and consolidation of the reading or writing insights learned in the earlier parts of the lesson. During the final ten minutes of the lesson, pupils were to be asked to reflect on their learning experiences and evaluate how successfully they had participated and improved.

This whole programme was completely revolutionary; nothing so directive had ever been imposed on English schools before. It also caused huge anxiety and many teachers felt, not surprisingly, utterly unprepared and vulnerable as they tentatively began their implementation of the Literacy Strategy in September 1998. Yet, extraordinarily, huge numbers of teachers, applying much goodwill and adapting their ideas in practical ways as they proceeded, discovered that it was a programme with the potential to bring about discernible positive change. A lot of pupils enjoyed the structure of the Literacy Hour; many, boys particularly, became motivated by the types of activity in which they were expected to participate; the pace of lessons increased and pupils became more confident about articulating what they had learned. Most significantly, the Strategy appeared to be improving standards of literacy, borne out by larger numbers of 11-year-old children attaining Level 4 in end of Key Stage 2 tests during subsequent years. By 2000, 75 per cent of pupils were entering Key Stage 3 at Level 4, the agreed national standard; almost 20 per cent more than the same year group had achieved in 1996.

The Strategy was not, of course, without its problems. A programme of such huge size and scale could not possibly be introduced without certain shortcomings, real or perceived. Some schools faced very real difficulties that hampered successful implementation, including poor learning behaviours, lack of purposeful management and teacher conservatism. Many teachers invested massive amounts of their spare time in finding necessary and appropriate textual resources to support learning in, sometimes, unfamiliar areas of study. Considerable numbers of primary teachers spent even more hours of supposedly 'free time' planning literacy lessons (and they still had the rest of the week with all the other attendant subjects to plan!). Understandable concerns were also expressed about pupils having insufficient time to finish pieces of writing, and teachers worried about contributing to promoting a culture where only textual extracts were studied, preventing the more customary and previously established practices of sustained reading of whole texts. 'Guided reading' and 'guided writing' were strange, demanding activities, and teachers were unsure about how to give real authority to the reflective 'plenary' sessions. The Hour, in its earliest days, was felt to be too inflexible, although most teachers began to experiment with its internal timings and content, until they discovered the arrangements that made them feel most comfortable.

Yet, four years on, the Literacy Strategy – now embodied in multiple versions of the Literacy Hour – is predominantly the means by which language and literacy are ostensibly taught in virtually every primary school in England. Nationally, primary teachers have established a clearer and more widely understood agenda about language and literacy teaching; they share a more common language around 'word, sentence and text level' objectives; they have raised considerably their expectations of what children are linguistically capable of achieving during the primary years; they plan much more purposefully to bring about more focused language learning outcomes and they are more confident and skilled about how to improve their pupils' reading and writing abilities.

Secondary developments

In a meeting of secondary Heads of English I organised in Oxford in 1997, I suggested to those colleagues who attended that they should take notice of the National Literacy Project, as the 'coming blueprint' for the teaching of English. But that early forecast soon appeared to be mistaken and misinformed. The Literacy Task Force report, published in August 1997, which was to impact so markedly on primary education, referred only sketchily to possible secondary developments, although it was recognised that secondary schools should 'build on the efforts of primary schools and work consistently across the curriculum to ensure that all pupils leave school confident in their understanding and use of written language' (DfEE 1997). Hidden away in paragraph 115, however, is the genesis of the current English and Literacy Strategies:

> On the basis of this investigation of good practice, we recommend that a small-scale GEST funded development programme on the lines of the National Literacy Project for primary schools is established to help secondary schools to improve literacy. The programme needs to have two strands. The first should deal with low standards of literacy at Key Stage 3 and be addressed primarily to English teachers and special educational needs and support staff. The second should be concerned

with the teaching of literacy within subjects throughout secondary schools. Both should be underpinned by a clear statement about the basis for effective teaching.

(DfEE 1997)

Without too much detailed explanation this paragraph begins to address the difficulties and tensions faced by secondary teachers, when considering the separate but related issues of *language* and *literacy* development, not regarded as problems in the same way by their primary counterparts. All secondary schools usually provide lessons in a subject called 'English', with particular emphasis on the reading and writing of textual material. Yet, the subject matter, areas of interest and components of that material will have only a marginal relationship with the reading and writing matter characteristic of the other separate subject areas, even though all that material is constituted in words and sentences in the English language. Indeed, paragraph 112 makes the specific point that: 'In shaping their plans it is essential that secondary schools do not see work on reading and writing as exclusively the province of a few teachers in the English and learning support departments' (DfEE 1997). This fundamental relationship between English and literacy will be explored in greater detail later on in this book.

Following the implementation of the primary Strategy in 1998, many English advisory and consultant staff grew increasingly concerned about the implications of the lack of clear progression into Key Stage 3. They applauded and continued to support the massive developments in primary practice, but saw no serious developments being prepared for Key Stage 3. Their worries were partially allayed in the summer term of 1999, when the National Literacy Strategy team set up a national programme of two-day conferences in every LEA, intended to involve all secondary schools to consider 'literacy across the curriculum' matters. The role of English departments in these arrangements was not wholly clear, and the overall approach of the supporting documentation was very tentative. A paragraph on 'Language and learning', in the conference folder, for instance, states:

> However, research by Wray and Lewis has shown that whilst most teachers recognise their responsibility in supporting the development of pupils' literacy skills, many feel unable to fulfil that responsibility. It is clear that colleagues in English and other departments need support in developing the expertise to maximise literacy learning opportunities in their lessons.

(DfEE 1999a)

Unfortunately, the conference file does not go on to suggest what that manner of 'support' might be.

In the event, the take-up by schools was only partial, and the school senior managers, on whose participation and interest such programmes were dependent, were not well represented. Most schools sent the Head of English and other English staff, and, in some cases, the Special Educational Needs Coordinator (SENCO). The Key Stage 3 'pilot' was not even in its infancy, and few materials specifically focused on secondary schools were available. Much of the time during these conferences was allocated to LEA literacy managers familiarising their secondary colleagues with the developments in the primary Strategy, sharing instances of local secondary good practice and encouraging school representatives to plan their future literacy action intentions. There was nothing striking or different with which to encourage secondary teachers to develop new responsibilities with regard to language and literacy teaching. It looked as though the momentum had slowed at that point.

Having made such a positive impression on primary 'standards', the Government, however, eventually turned its attention to secondary education. The evidence from Ofsted inspections and considerable educational research, notably that of Professor Jean Ruddock and her colleagues at Homerton College, Cambridge, suggested that Key Stage 3 required especial and extra attention. The youngest secondary pupils seemed, after their initial excitement of moving to the next phase, to lose their motivation and drive. Many pupils expressed their dissatisfaction at 'marking time'; too many progressed only one National Curriculum 'Level' in maths and English during that time, with a subsequent 'long tail of underachievement at Key Stage 4' (Ofsted 2000). Development from Key Stage 2 was not satisfactorily staged and supported. Some of the weakest teaching was seen with classes nationally in Years 7, 8 and 9. The literacy attainment of boys lagged significantly behind that of girls, and results at the end of Key Stage 3 were moribund. The problems were larger than merely pupil performance in literacy and numeracy, however; they were seen to be widespread, across the whole curriculum, and Ofsted suggested that many lessons in Key Stage 3 were failing to establish good foundations for later examination success:

> Despite these gradual improvements, six key concerns remain. First, National Curriculum Test results at Key Stage 3 remain too low. There has been some improvement in the mathematics results and a slight decline in English, but overall there has been relatively little change over the past five years. One third of pupils still lack the literacy and numeracy skills to reach Level 5.
>
> (Ofsted 2000)

Any new initiative to improve secondary results had to address more than just literacy and numeracy issues, although these elements would initially need to be seen as priorities. Therefore, when a secondary development programme was offered to some 200 schools, representing 17 diverse LEAs in the school year 1999/2000, it was based on intentions to bring about improvements in standards in Information and Communications Technology (ICT), science and the foundation subjects, as well as introducing new attitudes to cross-curricular approaches, such as 'thinking skills'. The 'literacy part' of this new Strategy was divided into two strands: a literacy across the curriculum strand and an English strand.

A number of different initiatives and interest groups were active, however, before the 'pilot' strategy, and their findings fed into the new programme. Her Majesty's Inspectorate (HMI) had been seeking and observing good cross-school literacy projects, then proliferating, and published their findings. The National Literacy Strategy Team, in its earliest stages comprising mostly former teachers and advisers with primary experience, began recruiting staff with a secondary background, and broadening its approach. Many English departments, impressed with the developments taking place in feeder primary schools, began – of their own volition – devising and exploring their own versions of secondary literacy programmes.

Then in the second half of the 1999/2000 school year a secondary English and literacy 'pilot' was officially launched. It was initially introduced into about 200 schools in 17 LEAs, building directly from lessons learned from the work taking place in primary schools, but not entirely a mirror image of that programme. The training was conducted, very speedily, in the summer of 2000, and on the basis of a model of support introduced in primary education (and acknowledging how much valuable support to schools had been lost through the former reduction of advisory teacher staff), Key Stage 3 Literacy Consultants were quickly appointed to carry forward the developments in their LEAs.

When David Blunkett addressed the prestigious North of England Education Conference in January 2001, to announce that the 'pilot' Strategy would be 'rolled out' nationally for all maintained secondary schools, the die was cast. All LEAs immediately advertised for leading English teachers to become Literacy Consultants to take forward the training and support in their area. This turned out to be a mixed blessing, leading to the recruitment of a huge group of extra trained staff, that removed, at a stroke, a whole generation of talented and enthused teachers from their classrooms! Local conferences and training were rapidly organised, and English departments prepared for the introduction of the English strand, in a context of growing whole-school awareness and imperative of addressing literacy issues in all subjects.

Valuable lessons had been learned from the 'pilot' Strategy, and the small, but growing, Key Stage 3 team at the National Literacy Strategy headquarters in Reading attempted to make the changes suggested from schools' experiences. The 'pilot' objectives, for instance, available on the Internet for nearly a whole school year, were gradually being adopted by considerably more schools than just those deemed 'pilot'. The objectives were reshaped and condensed, guided by the lessons learned in classrooms. 'Banks' of spelling, sentence level, and speaking and listening activities were collected and published. Huge folders of training materials were written and the infrastructure to enable national training programmes was put in place, made possible by Standards Funding. In the summer of 2001 English teachers, senior staff and colleagues from other subject areas attended training sessions conducted by LEA advisory teams, including their newly appointed Key Stage 3 Literacy Consultants. Every secondary school was required to devote a training day in the coming autumn term to disseminating and implementing the Literacy Across the Curriculum Programme.

2 The Key Stage 3 English *Framework*

Although all English departments are expected to implement the principles and objectives contained in the *Framework for Teaching English: Years 7, 8 and 9* (DfEE (Standards and Effectiveness Unit) 2001a) from September 2001, it is a process that will inevitably take some time to become even moderately successful. This book will attempt to assist English teachers as they confront major issues to do with anomalies between their current and future work, and will offer some possible suggestions for resolving them. English teaching is a partial procedure; it is not undertaken objectively or neutrally. My own prejudices and partialities will be evident as the book proceeds, although I hope that they will act as the starting points for further discussion, and not be simply rejected in those circumstances where they do not elicit immediate compatibility.

English teachers will in future have to address a number of related features, central to their work, that have been possible to avoid in the past, as they begin to make better sense of the Key Stage 3 English programme from September 2001, and relate it to the complementary scheme for cross-curricular literacy:

- It will be necessary to establish a view of the relationship between English and literacy in each school, and to share the characteristics of that relationship with other colleagues in the school, who are to be regarded as equal partners in overall literacy.
- English departments will be recommended to 'frame' their teaching and learning opportunities within the parameters of the 'four part lesson'.
- *All* teachers, but especially English teachers, will need to familiarise themselves with the contents of the *Framework for Teaching English: Years 7, 8 and 9*. They should become fully acquainted with the separate available objectives, to combine them in purposeful ways, likely to lead to the sorts of desirable language and literacy learning already agreed by the staff of the school.
- Although most English lessons have traditionally contained elements of 'word level', 'sentence level' and 'text level' considerations, it is expected in the new Strategy that they will in future be stressed separately, while the relationship between them is made more purposeful.
- English teachers will need to undertake training in, or at least refresh their knowledge of, grammar, phonics and spelling issues.

The *Framework* is a genuine departure from other, previous, ways of outlining learning in language and literacy in secondary schools in England. Indeed, there has been little 'other' material to compare with the contents of the *Framework*. Only since 1990, with the publication of the Programmes of Study in the National Curriculum Orders for English, has there been any sort of official documentation to outline what should be taught in the subject.

Subsequent revisions of National Curriculum documentation have become increasingly directive in specifying more precisely the range of literary texts to be studied in English classrooms. Yet, for all the growing centralisation of their subject, teachers of English have mostly been accustomed to choosing the contents of their courses without outside interference. They have certainly never before been confronted with specific objectives around which they will be expected to construct their teaching programmes.

Some teachers, unsurprisingly, are alarmed about having to build their future courses on such specific objectives imposed from a central agency. I hope to argue, in fact, that all departments will still retain enormous professional freedom even by adopting the Key Stage 3 *Framework*. While it contains objectives recommended by the NLS, these are firmly based on the sorts of assumptions currently to be found historically in the Schemes of Work published in hundreds of English departments. They are merely given greater attention and focus than they might currently attract, to specify to pupils and teachers alike the more precise nature of the literacy and language learning both groups ought to be seeking to achieve.

The relationship between the school subject 'English' and a broader, whole-school view of 'literacy'

Too many assumptions are made about the relative places of English and literacy in most schools. English teachers have not readily or regularly taken part in theoretical or philosophical discussions about the nature of their own subject and its contribution to pupils' language development. They have discussed this matter even less with colleagues from other subjects. Yet, it is the single most important component of the establishment of a successful language for learning programme in any secondary school.

Before worthwhile headway in addressing real language and literacy improvement can be made in English in any secondary school, it really is essential that all the teachers who work there devise a shared, straightforward insight into a notion of 'literacy'. It is quite impossible to state how vital this prerequisite should be in every school. The relationship between that whole-school understanding of 'literacy', how it will impact on each subject specialism and what those matters have to do with the work and concerns of the English department also should be clarified. If this relationship is not agreed, made clear, and published to guide all teachers, it is unlikely that any of the separate subject departments will make much real difference to the general literacy growth of their pupils. 'Literacy' – which is after all a cultural idea, having real currency where a community shares a common sense of it – can only flourish and become of worthwhile benefit to pupils if they encounter its fullest effects, on a regular basis and in the widest possible range of different learning contexts.

The *Framework for Teaching English: Years 7, 8 and 9* contains a number of references to 'literacy'. The most important is:

The notion of literacy embedded in the objectives is much more than simply the acquisition of 'basic skills' which is sometimes implied by the word: it encompasses the ability to recognise, understand and manipulate the conventions of language, and develop pupils' ability to use language imaginatively and flexibly.

(DfEE 2001a)

Most English teachers – indeed, probably all teachers – would recognise the good sense of this reference and have few problems using it as a starting point for discussions within their own departments, and with colleagues from other subjects. It unambiguously denies a 'reductionist' view of literacy, and it suggests that pupils should be empowered ('understand and manipulate the conventions of language') through these processes. Vitally, it also points to a creative outcome as one of the results of language study, making a necessary link with the literature so central to most definitions of the subject called English. It is an enormous improvement on the definition of literacy offered in the primary school *Framework for Teaching*, only three years previously: 'Literacy unites the important skills of reading and writing. It also involves speaking and listening' (DfEE 1998).

On the one hand, it is understandable why the NLS feared to tread too far into the complex debate about 'literacy', when its more immediate concerns were to implement the national programme, embodied in the Strategy, in a very limited period of time. On the other hand, by neglecting to offer some substantial working definitions of 'literacy', or even some acceptable, complementary alternatives, there has been a danger that teachers have not been guided sufficiently towards an acceptable, consensual view of what they might be attempting to achieve. The Strategy, as a consequence, also became more vulnerable to the condemnation of its critics, who were able to rework their representation of this initiative in any way that suited their arguments.

Undoubtedly, the view of 'literacy' projected in the primary Strategy is a narrow one. There is enormous concentration on six or seven non-fiction identifiable 'text types', with little regard to the ways those 'types' overlap and interweave in real textual contexts. Much attention is given to privileged sorts of reading: the nature of characters, and certain literary concerns, in rather isolated ways. Some of the more usual literacy learning contexts that pupils subconsciously encounter day-to-day, such as television, video and the popular magazine and publishing culture, are not successfully integrated, or even noticed. Virtually no regard is paid to the increasingly ubiquitous electronic technologies and their, as yet, undeveloped learning, communication and creative potentials. The 'literacy' central to the Strategy was also tightly linked with the ability to gain sufficient marks in a limited type of test, which in some not wholly defined way was supposed to be an indication of national standards!

There was, nevertheless, a strong imperative to make some kind of necessary change in the approaches being made to language learning, particularly in primary education, on a huge scale. Most of that change also depended on the efforts of non-specialists; very many teachers in Key Stages 1 and 2 were not trained teachers of English. While too much explanation, scholarship, rationale and, the dreaded word, 'theory', could well have been confusing, too little explanation has left the Strategy over exposed. Yet, a major component of literacy is undoubtedly to do with the teaching and learning of reading and writing. Traditionally, the subject called 'English' has been regarded as the forum in secondary schools most often concerned with teaching reading and writing, but that 'reading and writing' has usually been of a demarcated, specific kind. The textual materials mostly read and written in English have customarily been to do with what might broadly be described as 'the literary arts': a focused, rather small portion of literacy; possibly best characterised as 'literary literacy'. This particular focus has involved the reading of narrative fiction (some selected from the classical canon); poetry; drama and media texts (often as examples of 'persuasion'), with perhaps a few restricted instances of what has been quaintly described in the National Curriculum as 'literary' non-fiction (biography, travel writing etc.). By and large, pupils write or discuss critical and evaluative commentaries of their reading matter, occasionally producing examples of fictional prose (some of an empathetic nature, often embodying personal responses to fiction that has been read in their English lessons), occasionally engaging with poetry and drama scripts, and some passages of biography, recount and argument.

Secondary pupils experience only the most limited opportunities to write pieces of explanation, instructional text, non-chronological and other forms of report, evaluation, or description in their English lessons. Yet, the rest of the curriculum, taking up about 22 of their allocated 25 hours of in-school study each week, demands their confident proficiency in these and other text types. If they are not being taught and practising these text types in English, the only other circumstances for proper progression will be in the contexts, i.e. the other subjects, in which these genres should be appropriately employed. Geography, for instance, requires a considerable amount of reading and writing of explanation; geographers might, therefore, invest a portion of their teaching time enabling pupils to discover more about, practise and improve their skills of explanatory writing. Similarly, as instructional writing is frequently employed in science (e.g. how to conduct an experiment), teachers of science would use part of their lesson time profitably by pointing out, teaching and developing the important features of that type of text.

Too regularly definitions of 'literacy' are preceded by some sort of narrowing descriptor: *basic* or *functional* literacy, or *emotional* literacy, or even *school* literacy. These labels serve to deviate some of the central focus of worthwhile attention required in this difficult discussion. As Trevor Cairney reminds us: 'We acquire specific literacy in rich social contexts as we engage in unique sets of human relationships. Because literacy is socially defined and sustained, individuals come to literacy in slightly different ways' (Cairney 1995).

Cairney goes on to argue that 'literacy' is not a single literacy skill. (It is worth noting how we have trouble representing the word 'literacy'; is it literacy, Literacy, 'literacy' or *literacy*?) Literacy practices will be dependent on certain sorts of literacy environments. If schools concentrate on a narrow, 'basic skills' type of approach to this topic, they will be likely to concentrate on spelling and punctuation, on decoding and 'correct' speaking. This very reductionist view has been the particular representation preferred by the detractors of the Strategy, regularly writing over-dramatically in *The Times Education Supplement (TES)*. The Government, unfortunately, reinforces this view when it wraps up and 'spins' its Strategies in economic imperatives, linking them inextricably to numerical targets and league tables, rather than expressing them in human growth terms and, possibly, with the capability of bringing about a changed society.

English teachers come from a background with regard to learning about language where the arguments and justifications offered by various Secretaries of State find little sympathy. 'Literacy', as defined in the official documentation, has not been related closely to the more personal, 'enjoyment' agenda, in line with what takes place in the majority of English lessons. The texts selected for study in English are often regarded as the 'training' materials to encourage the growth of personal reflection, contemplation and an increasing understanding of human experiences, through the imaginative ways in which they illuminate instances of our shared existence, as their stock-in-trade. That context for textual insight and understanding is clearly at odds with the literacy shorthand of the Government aspiring to achieve the much sought after Level 4 for the vast majority! So, thinking has to be constructed around the notion of 'literacy', capable of challenging the formerly mutually exclusive definitions. I offer this starting point:

> Literacy is the capability of recognising the nature of, responding appropriately to and feeling confident with controlling and making meanings within the widest possible range of discourses in the many linguistic contexts we encounter.

It is a rough and ready 'draft' working definition: the beginning of an exploration of this difficult problem, not its solution. But if this sort of discussion is taking place as a backdrop to the introduction of both English and literacy across the curriculum in the Key Stage 3 Strategy, then real progress is likely to be more possible. Figure 2.1 was devised in my LEA to help a sceptical secondary senior manager sort out what he regarded as confusing differences between 'literacy', 'language' and 'English', as a preliminary to introducing 'literacy' in his school. Whilst it helped to discriminate between those separate ideas, it also pointed up the areas where those three topics overlapped.

All secondary schools have been recommended to, and really ought to, carry out a *literacy audit*, or similar review, as part of their preparation for the literacy training programme, by identifying the current strengths and requirements in respect of each department's literacy procedures. An audit booklet was made available in the School Management Pack at the launch of the Strategy, capable of being applied to all curriculum subjects. The likelihood is, unfortunately, that this analytical instrument will be employed more thoroughly in some schools than in others. Its intention is to help teachers, who mostly have never before had to reflect in depth on these matters, to realise the multidimensional characteristics of literacy across the school. As Figure 2.2 shows (see page 14), each subject area contains intrinsic literacy practices and problems particular to itself, but some issues are shared, and where such generic concerns occur they can be tackled more successfully if all staff of the school are aware of them and their interrelatedness.

Every department should be asking itself at least the following very straight-forward questions:

- How much reading by pupils is expected in our work, and for what purposes?
- How much teaching of reading is planned and carried out?
- What sorts of writing do we expect of our pupils?
- How much teaching of writing is planned and actually carried out?
- How are pupils' literacy skills expected to support their learning in our subject, and how ought we to set about improving those skills?

Literacy	Language	English
The fullest insight into the 'languages' culture in which we live –	The 'material'/components of ALL texts	The name of the language.
The total repertoire of controlled, appropriate and purposeful EXPRESSION (speaking & writing) or MEANING MAKING (listening & reading) across the whole range of social and learning discourses embodied in TEXTS	words/phrases/clauses/sentences signs/symbols images gestures	A school subject, defined through National Curriculum Orders/historical practice **– in Key Stage 1** usually (pre NLS) meaning initial instruction in reading & writing of all mostly fiction texts (some speaking & listening) – recently broader range of texts **– in Key Stage 2** usually (before NLS) increasingly concerned with literary texts (narrative fiction/poetry/a little drama – personal recount/descriptive writing) – and some non-fiction study as part of growing literacy knowledge **– in Key Stages 3 & 4** usually about increasing attention on literary texts – poetic/metaphoric/dramatic – classical literary canon – some study of modern fiction/media texts – increasingly critical/evaluative writing – some personal/imaginative, argument/reasoning writing (imagine/explore/entertain inform/explain/describe persuade/argue/advise analyse/review/comment)
	ways of conveying meaning through agreed culturally based linguistic structures in purposeful discourses called TEXTS	
So – in practice – if purpose is to **instruct** that usually means that the text will:	be constructed in imperative voice (2nd person) be in present tense be in sequential development be in short, pointed sentences	
– if purpose is to **describe**		
that usually means that the text will contain:	many adjectives/adverbs adjectival/adverbial phrases metaphors and similes viewpoint in 1st/3rd person/past or present tense	

– if purpose is to **narrate**

that usually means that the text will:
be written in 1st/3rd person
be in the past tense
have variable sentence length (genre dependent)
possibly include dialogue

So – within our literacy culture – there are huge numbers of **text types** intended to fulfil particular purposes, by employing linguistic devices in particular ways.

They might be: describing/persuading/reflecting/commenting/explaining/recounting/evaluating/exploring/abusing/inciting etc.

Some are narrating stories or events in order to: excite (action adventure)/move (love)/impress (describe)/frighten (horror)/amuse (comedy)/tease (suspense)/forecast (science fiction)/reflect (war).

Learning is intrinsically bound up and contained/framed in the discourses in which it takes place.
An example – in Chemistry – could see the pupil possibly expected to:

inform the teacher of specific facts
recount the details of an experiment
explain what has taken place in a chemical reaction
describe what was seen as a result of the reaction
evaluate how successful an experiment might have been

} all different linguistic tasks – involving separate/distinguishable grammars – fulfilling different purposes

Figure 2.1 The differences between 'literacy', 'language' and 'English'

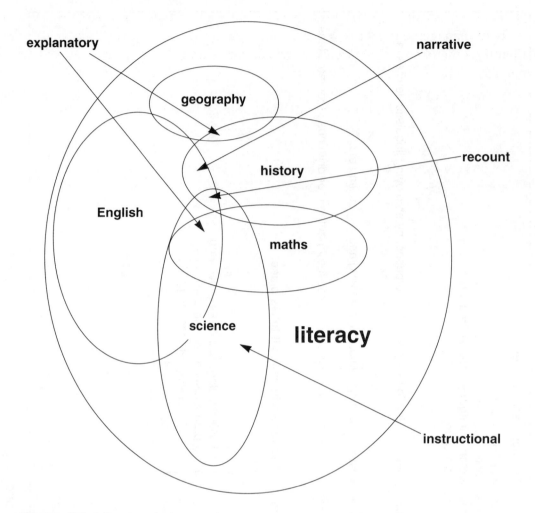

Figure 2.2 Literacy circle

Without intending to embarrass anybody, before September 2001 it would have been likely that virtually every subject department in the country would not have been able to provide a very detailed answer to any of these questions. In fairness to those departments, there has been little leadership or projected sense of possible improvement, in terms of developing literacy and language skills, promoted by Senior Management Teams with the staffs of their schools.

After years of working alongside schools attempting to address issues of whole-school literacy, I have become convinced that the full commitment of the Senior Management Team is an essential prerequisite if the initiative is to have any chance of success. When challenged by a senior member of staff (ideally the head teacher or the deputy head teacher with responsibility for the curriculum), about the sorts of questions suggested above, departments would have to begin changing their attitudes to literacy. The Government and those responsible for the Key Stage 3 Strategy also stress this point equally clearly. In a booklet supplied to all schools, *Management Guide: Lessons from the Pilot* (DfEE 2001b), addressed directly to head teachers by their peers who had experienced the pilot Strategy, is the following advice: 'We knew that we and our senior managers would play a central role in making things happen, and that we would need to promote the Strategy and give it our constant backing' (p. 4); 'Like most of the pilot schools we identified a formal Strategy management group and a senior manager to coordinate the work' (p. 5); 'Identify a member of your senior management team to act as Key Stage 3 Strategy manager and to chair a management group' (p. 5); 'Give the Strategy your full backing and spell out what you expect it to achieve in your school' (p. 26). Many schools have learned, through wasted investment of time and energy in previous attempts, that leaving literacy developments solely in the keeping of a junior member of staff (the second-in-charge of the English department is often that person!) will not lead to real development, a shared understanding by the whole staff or any sense of whole-school priority; however dedicated that teacher might be.

The *Framework for Teaching English: Years 7, 8 and 9* states:

> English teachers have a leading role in providing pupils with the knowledge, skills and understanding they need to read, write, speak and listen effectively, *but this document also addresses other subject staff*. Language is the prime medium through which pupils learn and express themselves across the curriculum, *and all teachers have a stake in effective literacy*.
>
> (DfEE 2001a, emphasis added)

This seemingly innocuous paragraph is extremely important and its implications demand proper attention in all schools.

Historically, the development of 'Language Across the Curriculum', as this sort of programme is usually known, has been bedevilled by mutual misunderstandings. Teachers of other subjects have commonly believed that how well pupils read, write, discuss and spell has to do with what takes place in English lessons. English teachers have attempted to point out to their colleagues that English is not 'a service industry' (as I have actually heard it named) to the other subjects; it has its own discrete concerns. Yet, they have been unable to describe just what ought to be taking place in those other subjects to complement their own teaching, and to contribute to the sort of positive literacy environment likely to allow pupils to grow satisfactorily as language users.

A second difficulty has been to do with the ways less able pupils have been supported in many lessons. It is now an accepted fact that the underachievement of many pupils is often due to their poor literacy skills. Unable to find their way into the language of specific subjects, to make worthwhile conceptual involvement, they are then limited in the expression of what learning they might have acquired because their writing abilities are undeveloped. Too often these pupils have been withdrawn from lessons, or are given worksheets or simplified alternative programmes that fail to re-engage them sufficiently rigorously. These sorts of tactics tend to avoid facing the problems of poor literacy, rather than enabling pupils to confront and remediate them. Such pupils remain on the fringes of involvement, with no means of making progress. Where all the teachers in a school have collaboratively formulated an approach to literacy, such mistakes are less likely to happen and more pupils can be brought back into a fully supportive learning culture.

Finally, but extremely important in the changed context from September 2001, English teachers in secondary schools face a particular difficulty that is not seen as a problem by other teaching colleagues but does directly affect them. At the end of Key Stage 3 all pupils in Year 9 take a test called 'English', which, in some not wholly specified way, is also an assessment of their broad 'literacy' abilities. English teachers only have control of part of the learning process contributing to those abilities; their pupils' broader literacy skills are acquired through many sorts of textual engagement, some of which take place in, but many others beyond, the school. Sharing a view of literacy with all colleagues will, at least, begin to ensure that pupils are receiving common messages about the ways they can improve, practise and most effectively use their skills in school. English teachers can also be more assured that their pupils' skills are being developed in line with the requirements of the test, which is likely to enhance results in all subjects.

Page 10 of the Key Stage 3 *Framework for Teaching English* specifies some ambitious 'sophisticated literacy skills' intended as the 'overall aims' resulting from its adoption. These 'literacy skills' also have implications for teachers other than English staff, if the pupils are to begin successfully utilising such skills and achieving in all their textual engagements. The *Framework* states: By the end of Year 9 we expect each pupil to be a shrewd and fluent independent reader:

- orchestrating a range of strategies to get at meaning in text, including inferential and evaluative skills;
- sensitive to the way [sic] meanings are made; (DfEE 2001a)

Even allowing for the mistake of suggesting just one way of 'making meaning', these are very complex and demanding requirements, necessitating an understanding by all the teachers with whom they are to come into contact if the pupils are to achieve anything like that goal. Similarly, 'a confident writer' should be 'able to write for a variety of purposes and audiences, knowing the conventions and beginning to adapt and develop them' (DfEE 2001a). So, pupils are not only expected to 'know the conventions', but they should be using that complex writing knowledge as the starting point for even further progress. Perhaps it means such skills as understanding the relationship, for instance, between instructional text and explanatory text so well that pupils are able to rewrite the contents of one text type in the manner of the other. That would indeed be a very 'sophisticated literacy' accomplishment.

The three 'skills' quoted in the preceding paragraph offer the potential for a genuinely challenging language INSET programme for any school. If all members of staff could be helped to explore and learn what is truly meant by 'orchestrating a range of strategies to get at meaning in text', or could develop their pupils' abilities to increase their powers of becoming 'sensitive to the way[s] meanings are made', it would be possible to change positively the approaches to reading in their classrooms.

Similarly, if all teachers, promoting the skills of being 'able to write for a variety of purposes and audiences', insisted on pupils regularly prefacing their significant writing exercises with some consideration of the *purpose* of the piece, and devoted a few moments of discussion to considering the *most appropriate text type* in which it ought to be composed, then they could truly transform the quality of classroom writing. It is in such straightforward and simple acts of collaborative teaching methodologies that significant improvement can be brought about.

Perhaps most tellingly, the criteria for becoming 'an effective speaker and listener' can and ought to be applied to most learning activities taking place in any subject area. According to the *Framework*, the effective speaker and listener:

- [has] the clarity and confidence to convey a point of view or information;
- uses talk to explore, create, question and revise ideas, recognising language as a tool for learning;
- is able to work effectively with others in a range of roles;
- has a varied repertoire of styles, which are used appropriately.

(DfEE 2001a)

Supporting and developing these skills in all subjects would feed into and improve the reading and writing attainment of all pupils, as well as creating a more demanding and secure talk learning culture.

I want to make one strong recommendation at this stage of considering literacy across the curriculum. It has to do with the role of teachers of modern languages. This group of staff is often not included specifically in discussions about how to make literacy skills more manifest across the whole school, and yet, to some extent, they have been the most obvious teachers of 'language' issues for years! They have certainly been the group responsible for keeping any study of grammar alive. To help pupils understand the way language works in their native tongue, it can often be helpful to compare certain parts with those same linguistic elements employed in other languages. English teachers will be asked to teach grammar skills and emphasise 'sentence level' knowledge more obviously in the new Strategy. These would be more effectively taught if they were aligned with some of the objectives teachers of French, or Spanish, or German, for instance, were including in their lessons. These are early days in the development of shared grammar and linguistic learning objectives, but English staff might be helped enormously in their own preparation for this new area of their work if assisted more closely by their modern languages colleagues. Surprisingly, the Strategy manuals make no reference to the obvious involvement and special contribution potentially possible by modern languages colleagues. This potential needs to be recognised and developed by schools.

The necessity of developing the English Key Stage 3 'strand' in relation to literacy across the curriculum

The English 'strand' of the Key Stage 3 Strategy will not improve pupils' overall literacy and language attainment in isolation. English teachers, through their own devices, could bring about some gains in their pupils' critical skills, close reading abilities, their writing achievement and some speaking and listening accomplishments, *in a limited set of contexts*, but not overall. They simply do not have the necessary time, and the contents of their particular subject curriculum would not make such extensive ambitions possible. English teachers, therefore, have a vested interest in helping and supporting their colleagues in other subjects to learn more about literacy, and then urging them to share that learning with all pupils.

Page 10 of the *Framework for Teaching English: Years 7, 8 and 9* makes this relationship completely clear:

English teachers have a leading role in providing pupils with the knowledge, skills and understanding they need to read, write, speak and listen effectively, *but this document also addresses other subject staff.* Language is the prime medium through which pupils learn and express themselves across the curriculum, and all teachers have a stake in effective literacy.

(DfEE 2001a, emphasis added)

In December 1975, the Department of Education and Science published a seminal document, *A Language for Life* (DES 1975), more commonly known as the 'Bullock Report' after the name of its Chairman, Sir Alan Bullock. The Report contained 333 recommendations, many concerned with important ways of improving literacy skills across the curriculum. It was widely admired, considered to be a work of impressive scholarship, and welcomed by politicians, a wide range of educationalists and English teachers alike. Yet, while this report influenced policies of many schools, it was ultimately unable to bring about any practical change in the ways teachers of all subjects addressed the issues of literacy in their lessons. The recommendations were very worthy, and still seem very sensible when seen in print, as selective quotations illustrate:

3. Every school should devise a systematic policy for the development of reading competence in pupils of all ages and ability levels.

125. The teacher should extend the pupil's ability as a writer primarily by developing his [sic] intentions and then by working on the techniques appropriate to them.

131. The ability to spell should be regarded as part of the common responsibility for language development, which should be shared by teachers of all subjects.

138. In the secondary school, all subject teachers need to be aware of:

(i) the linguistic processes by which their pupils acquire information and understanding, and the implications for the teacher's own use of language;
(ii) the reading demands of their own subjects, and ways in which the pupils can be helped to meet them. (DES 1975)

But very few teachers (English teachers included), knew how to translate such recommendations into planning and teaching activities at that time.

Other factors preventing the Bullock Report making a real difference were:

1. while the Government had sponsored and supported the Report, it did not invest further money to ensure its understanding and adoption;
2. it was not translated into government policy;
3. even though most senior managers in schools approved of the Report's sentiments and intentions, they did not appoint themselves to the whole-school coordination roles as recommended by the Report, but usually expected a member of the English department to fulfil that function;
4. it was perceived in most schools as an initiative in the remit of the English department, and teachers of other subjects were never made fully aware of their own association with literacy;
5. most English departments, at that time, taught language skills cursorily and with great reluctance, or prescriptively;

6. no time was set aside for training all teachers in the school:
7. where the Report led to developments in school policy documentation, it was rarely identified as part of the priority action programme;
8. there were insufficient LEA staff able to assist schools and translate the document into practical in-school guidance.

So, what has changed? How is the situation so different in 2001 that there is a greater likelihood of achieving the wholesale transformation in the attitudes and practices of all secondary schools the Government seeks, through the implementation of the Key Stage 3 Strategy?

First, the Strategy is central to government policy, and is underpinned by sophisticated and demanding target-setting procedures that are being carried out simultaneously in all secondary schools.

- Schools and their LEAs are being held very accountable, and have to prove that they are using the Standards Funds resources, intended to pay for change and development, in efficient and focused ways.
- A network of Key Stage 3 Literacy Consultants has been appointed, under the dual supervision of Literacy Regional Directors and LEA Literacy Managers, to support and challenge schools in their developmental programmes.
- A common national training programme has been published, and money provided for teachers to be released from their classrooms to familiarise themselves with the materials.
- The monitoring agencies, such as Ofsted, are expecting to see that these developments have taken place, and will be evaluating how successfully they believe individual schools are contributing to national improvements.

Secondly, and just as importantly, we know more about the way pupils learn language and become more literate than we did at the publication of the Bullock Report. It is now possible to involve all teachers in a shared enterprise to improve standards in literacy across the curriculum as more tangible information and assistance can be supplied to them, which they will find they can integrate in their own work.

English teachers also approach their work in a different manner than they would have done in 1975. The culture of increased accountability in education generally, manifested in the adoption of such details as Schemes of Work, and a greater awareness of the necessity of articulating more precisely the intended ways of bringing about learning in 'English', have considerably changed teaching attitudes in the subject. The experiences of the primary Literacy Strategy have also challenged some long-held prejudices and beliefs of English teachers, who have seen the pace of lessons increase and the focus sharpen in infant and junior classrooms. Secondary teachers have also realised that younger pupils have a capacity for learning and using linguistic and grammatical information to ask more pithy questions of their reading, and to apply in improving their writing, than had been previously recognised.

The research on functional grammar, or genre study, undertaken by M. A. K. Halliday (Halliday and Hasan 1989) has pointed up the need for those concerned with the teaching of language to pay greater attention to the *purposes* of *whole texts*, particularly whole non-fiction texts, when exploring how they work. Halliday's work, supported by the research of Beverley Derewianka (Derewianka 1990), Alison Littlefair (Littlefair 1991) and Gunter Kress (Kress 1989) among others, has suggested a strong case for recognising that *the grammatical structures of texts are dependent on their intentions*. So, *the ways texts are structured have clear relationships with the functions those texts are supposed to be performing.*

> If we have some linguistic understanding of how writers choose language for their varying purposes we have valuable insights which can greatly inform our teaching of both reading and writing across the curriculum. It is not sufficient simply to expose all children to a wide range of texts. We have to help young readers not only to read the content of the text but also to become aware of how the content is organised. In other words our concern is to teach children how language varies as we read and write for different purposes.
>
> (Littlefair 1992)

This sort of information is invaluable for understanding how to teach literacy, and this area of linguistic research has contributed strongly to the literacy strand of the Strategy. It also offers a further dimension to departments that have tentatively begun to support their pupils' literacy learning, but have little idea of how to proceed beyond their good intentions and few, unconnected activities.

'Word level', 'sentence level' and 'text level' issues in literacy across the curriculum

Many subject departments in hundreds of schools have long been aware of the important role they could potentially play in improving their pupils' learning if they also paid greater attention to the ways language is employed in their studies. On the walls of their classrooms some have published *subject-related vocabulary lists*, to use as aide-mémoires for their pupils in their written tasks, and to improve spelling of those terms. Some also use *subject wordbooks* to support pupils more systematically as they encounter new and unfamiliar subject-related vocabulary, and to encourage pupils to pay greater, independent attention to the words of texts.

These sorts of examples of support, however, are often as far as most departments have gone in their programmes to enhance literacy across the curriculum. They certainly offer a worthwhile start to such an enterprise, but they have only restricted powers of making pupils more competent and skilled in their textual engagements. Paying most attention to the separate fragments of texts will not, in the long run, assist pupils to make more than just a portion of the available meaning, and their reading and writing strategies are not much improved as a consequence.

The *Framework* Teaching Objectives for Years 7, 8 and 9, which can be found on pages 22–32 of the publication (DfEE 2001a), are grouped into 'word level', 'sentence level' and 'text level' sections. Primary teachers have become familiar with these terms during the three years of the Literacy Strategy – as have their pupils – but they will not be natural ways of categorising language and literacy learning for many secondary teachers.

Why 'word level', 'sentence level' and 'text level' divisions?

Linguists have been using the subdivisions 'word level', 'sentence level' and 'text level' for a long time. Roger Beard in his *National Literacy Strategy: Review of Research and Other Related Evidence* claims:

> The word/sentence/text level distinctions are a convenient way of referring to the visual features of what we read and write and are helpful in providing consistent points of reference for teachers and pupils when talking about the processes and products of literacy learning.
>
> (Beard 1998)

He goes on to quote David Crystal (1995), who makes a distinction in a diagram of English between 'text' (a coherent self-contained unit of discourse), 'grammar' (the system of rules governing the construction of sentences) and 'lexicon' (the vocabulary of a language). It is not, as Beard reminds us, a perfect set of distinctions:

> For instance, grammatical rules apply *within* words (morphology) as well as *between* words (syntax). Meaning is conveyed at word level (vocabulary) as well as at discourse or text level. Punctuation is part of the graphology but also plays an important role in confirming the grammatical rules which are being used.
>
> (Beard 1998)

These divisions help to articulate some important 'models' of teaching reading and writing, which have sometimes not been defined as a basis of language learning, even by English departments. The primary Literacy Strategy is premised on the 'searchlight' model as shown in Figure 2.3.

This could be moderately helpful for secondary teachers, but it is, not unreasonably, a 'political' model rather heavily emphasising the very obvious incorporation of phonics (an important issue at the time of the introduction of the Literacy Strategy). Much the same message can be conveyed in Figure 2.4, which includes some valuable insights about the 'knowledges' required about learning how to read, much of it

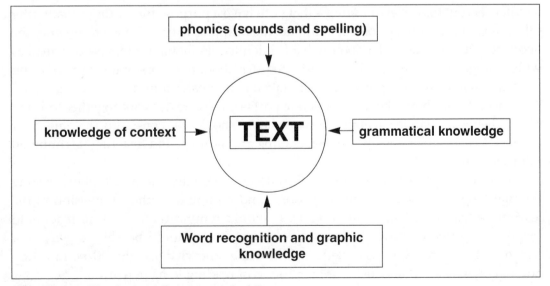

Figure 2.3 The 'searchlight' model of literacy

Readers and writers need to grasp and relate the following 'knowledges' to improve their literacy skills:

R E A D I N G ↑

SEMANTIC KNOWLEDGE (Text level)
(The nature of texts – fiction/non-fiction – text types/genres – purpose of text – reason for reading/writing – study/pleasure – previous experience of text, etc.)

SYNTACTICAL KNOWLEDGE (Sentence level)
(The grammatical knowledge of texts – how the language works/relationships of words in sentences/paragraphs to establish purpose – presentational features – punctuation)

GRAPHO-PHONOLOGICAL KNOWLEDGE (Word level)
(Relating sounds to letter symbols – blending words – patterns of spelling – morphology – vocabulary)

W R I T I N G ↓

Reading requires decoding of symbols, to make words which relate in sentences, to make up texts. *Writing* is deciding on a text/genre to construct, choosing the correct relationship and patterning of words in sentences, themselves built up from symbols representing sounds.

Figure 2.4 The 'knowledges' required for relating reading and writing

derived from the research of Marilyn Jager Adams, and her team, included in *Beginning to Read* (Adams 1990).

In essence, Figure 2.4 is making explicit the *intrinsic relationship between reading and writing,* such a powerful tool in teaching primary children how to develop textual and linguistic understanding. Essentially, reading and writing are the same thing! They merely approach texts and textual meaning from different directions. In our culture there are thousands of social discourses, each with their own linguistic arrangements, some only differing slightly from others, but each with its own distinct nuances. When a writer sets out to convey meaning – that is, to have a purpose for writing – that writer selects an appropriate type of text to 'frame' the meaning with real power, and offer the necessary clues to the reader about what is intended. Potential writers need to read as wide a range of texts as possible, in order to learn about the types of text available and to ensure that the writing process is undertaken with greater confidence and assurance. They need to be shown how the separate parts of those texts work together to bring about their cumulative, overall effects. Schools should be constantly helping their pupils to see this relationship between reading and writing, and fostering its continual improvement.

The approach presented in Figure 2.4 could be an equally valuable tool in assisting the planning of secondary English lessons, and adding a further dimension to the learning intentions of all other subjects. It should remind us that for all readers to make any sort of worthwhile meaning of a text, they should be able to activate a number of simultaneous 'knowledges'. All those 'knowledges' should be in action and interacting simultaneously for the process of reading to have real validity.

Grapho-phonological knowledge (attaching sounds to written marks) – the word level

In reading a piece of published text (i.e. words imprinted on some form of surface) the reader quite obviously has to be able to *decode*. The eye lights on squiggles to which sounds are ascribed and agreed in our literacy culture. The English language presents difficulties for many readers because there are 26 letters, but approximately (it cannot be precisely stated for all readers, because local dialects can make differences) 44 sounds. So, to illustrate the sorts of complications this causes, the 'ph' of 'phonic' is said like the 'f' in 'fish. While readers are coping with recognising the 'little pictures' – which is what the letters are, they also have to make decisions about the possible alternative sounds presented by some: is the 'c' soft as in 'cite', or hard as in 'clot'?

These sounds are then blended to make words. Most of those words (called 'lexical' words) have some form of intrinsic meaning. The 'grammatical' words, the connectors, are harder to attach meaning to until they are functioning in bigger units of text. Even some 'lexical' words will only reveal their meaning when that word is seen 'in use' in a sentence, juxtaposed with other words offering a helpful context. The word can also take on specific meanings in specialised settings: 'field' has different meanings for a geographer and a physicist. Some pupils are unable to access meaning at word level because they have never been acquainted with that particular vocabulary. They will, in turn, need other forms of assistance before being able to employ their other reading knowledges. For instance, words beginning with, or containing the letters 'hydro' will have a meaning indicating something to do with water.

Mostly, however, a reader uses the decoding process to access and sound out sets of words to put together in sentences; competent, experienced readers use this skill, usually without a thought, until an unfamiliar word crops up in a passage calling for a pause and a longer investigation. Good readers expect to assimilate their decoding capabilities within a multidimensional approach to reading, and once they are fluent, the phonemic capacity assumes less importance.

Part of the decoding process is, of course, based on an increasing use of phonemic understanding. When readers are sometimes stumped by a word, they often break it down into sections (syllables) and say the sounds they are able to recognise in those parts, then they combine those sounds to reconstruct the whole word. One of the features of the English strand of the Strategy will be the growing reliance pupils are expected to develop in phonics to more thoroughly underpin their improved spelling capabilities. Good readers also use the contexts of their reading for identifying and pinning down the meanings of unfamiliar vocabulary.

Syntactical knowledge (from 'syntax' – the grammar of the sentence) – the sentence level

In the English language most meaning is conveyed through the specific arrangements of words, known as sentences, less on the actual word endings (as is more usual in French, German, or Latin). Take the example of the word 'running' appearing by itself, without a surrounding helpful context. It could be the present participle of a verb, 'I am running' or the name of the activity, 'Press-ups will be followed by running.' Alternatively, it could be placed in front of a noun to become an adjective, such as 'running shoe'. Only by 'putting the word into action' is it possible to identify its meaning.

More significantly for teachers, however, is the realisation that certain sorts of sentence serve particular purposes. A sentence *instructing* someone or something is likely to:

1. have its verb placed early in the sentence, sometimes as the very first word;
2. be in the simple present tense;
3. be constructed in the second person, imperative voice;
4. be short and to the point, without unnecessary decoration or detail.

These 'facts' of writing can be made available to pupils so they become more accomplished in recognising and enquiring about the structural devices they are employing.

> Rothery (1984) suggests that children can be effectively introduced to specific genres of writing. Such a proposal is not purely formulaic. Rather it is a teaching strategy which enables children to extend their awareness of writing strategies. In other words children should be aware of their options and be able to discuss forms of writing which are appropriate for their purposes.
>
> (Littlefair 1992)

The linguist George Keith characteristically offers lively, relevant examples of the ways syntactical knowledge can bring about greater textual understanding in both fiction and non-fiction reading, by pupils acquiring the skills of probing sentence structuring, and using this knowledge confidently as a supportive aid in their writing:

> Think about the increased control over their writing pupils can gain from being aware that the same paragraph could begin with a question or a command as well as a statement. Yet think how sublimely pointless pronouns and sentence functions could be made in English lessons. If, on the other hand, pronouns were tackled by investigating them in use, classifying their uses and experimenting with them in pupils' own texts – what a difference! Similarly, question sentences could be explored: 'Where are they best placed in texts? Why is the question and answer format so popular in informative texts cum persuasive writing? Do readers really like having their supposed questions answered for them?' Again, what a difference in the teaching approach!
>
> (Keith 1997)

George Keith has, in that one paragraph, not only justified why sentence level, syntactic knowledge is a necessary reading and writing tool, but also embodied a whole positively focused teaching approach in the spirit of the Strategy.

Semantic knowledge (text level knowledge)
Genre study has done much to reposition attention in language studies on to the whole text. Semantic knowledge concerns those parts of a reader's understanding that focus on context, purpose, and overall appropriateness of single texts, aligning with others sharing similar characteristics, and contrasting them with those with significant differences. To know about texts means needing to know about the ways texts work in the world. From the beginning of their engagements with written texts, readers usually begin to discriminate between different story texts. They soon tell the

difference between certain tales, for example, featuring people in their plots, and those involving animals. It is also possible for young readers to recognise the differences between fiction and non-fiction (as the Literacy Strategy has demonstrated), and as those readers gain further skills they learn how to categorise more discriminatingly those non-fiction texts, and find appropriate uses for them.

Genre knowledge also offers pupils a way into a fuller language engagement, in reading and writing situations:

> The main purpose of a curriculum genre is to teach about the way language works within a genre rather than concentrating on pupils' cognitive response to a task. The curriculum genre involves modelling, teaching of structure, joint negotiation of text, consultation on a one-to-one basis and on a group basis. The consultation is about language rather than the pupils' personal input; it is a means of discussing with pupils the development of their language skills. Once pupils have understood the shape of a genre, then they can use it creatively and begin to understand the creative manipulation of it by others. This is hardly the teaching of sterile formulae.
>
> (Littlefair 1991)

This way of working with texts is utterly central to the understanding and interpretation of the English and literacy 'strands' of the Key Stage 3 Strategy. English teachers will also recognise the components of the 'four part English lesson' as recommended in the *Framework*, and dealt with in greater detail in Chapter 3.

To put it simply, *readers* go through a process where their eyes alight on the letters of the page to which they attach sounds. They blend the sounds into contextually sensible combinations, making words that form sentences structured in characteristic ways, recognisable as examples of particular sorts of text, fulfilling particular purposes. Of course, fluent readers do not read in this mechanistic, hierarchical way; their experience enables these knowledges to interact simultaneously. For instance, their knowledge of the text type will be guiding the way they blend sounds to make the appropriate words, and their expectations of structural devices of a text type allow them to make rapid progress through the text.

Writers, however, set off to create a text of a specific kind, intending to fulfil a clear purpose. They have to create sentences, structured in ways best suited to conveying those intentions, by calling on and placing the most relevant words in a particular order.

At every stage of the writing process a writer will be making decisions about:

- whether the text type, or combinations of different types of texts, is capable of providing the correct framing device for the purpose;
- the order and length of the sentences;
- the best vocabulary capable of conveying the clearest meaning and effects to a known audience.

English departments will probably not have spent as much time in the past discriminating between these areas of textual knowledge, and separating them for teaching and learning purposes quite so obviously. Ronald Carter (1988) suggests that reactionary and romantic opinion characterise debates about teaching English in Britain. One of the ways in which he sees possible development from such polarisation is through the Australian work on genres and curricular genres. He describes genres as occupying 'a curricular space between reactionaryism and romanticism: between language as a creative resource and language as patterned regularity' (Carter 1988). Similarly, Alison Littlefair argues that:

> A genre-based model of teaching language should not be seen in opposition to a personal development model; rather the two models can be seen as complementary. If we polarize the purposes of the two models, then we ignore the importance of a flexible approach to teaching language to pupils who inevitably have varying needs.

> (Littlefair 1991)

Word level study in the English lesson

A quick glance at pages 22–32 of the *Framework*, outlining the learning objectives pupils are expected to cover in Years 7, 8 and 9, will make clear to any teacher that 'Word level' matters are intended to be regarded more seriously in the future as an important category of learning. The *Framework* consistently divides them, in all three years, into 'Spelling', 'Spelling strategies' and 'Vocabulary' subsections. The first two subheadings are worth considering in detail, as many English teachers would not have been confident teaching these aspects of the subject in the past. Once again, however, it is necessary to stress that *these objectives are not necessarily the sole responsibility of the English department*! Indeed separate objectives in Years 7 and 8 emphasise this very point:

> Year 7 – Pupils should revise, consolidate and secure:
> 7. the spellings of key words in each subject.
> Year 8 –
> 9. appreciate the precise meaning of specialist vocabulary for each school subject, and use specialist terms aptly in their own writing;

> (DfEE 2001a: 22, 27)

The principles and learning approaches contained in these objectives would be far more effective if understood and practised by all teachers in the school. (Indeed, if all the teachers in their literacy training were able to be acquainted with the Year 7 Progress Unit booklet on 'Spelling' (DfEE 2001h), then the school could really begin to adopt a substantially based shared approach to this topic.) A 'starter' list of suggested subject-related words is supplied in the *Framework* folder, on pages 48–53. When these were first published, critics of the Strategy took mischievous delight in mistakenly claiming that these were 'compulsory government spelling lists' and raging against them.

Spelling lists scorned as 'control freakery'
Secondary schools reacted angrily this week as the Government issued lists of more than 700 key words that they believe every child of 14 should be able to spell . . . They prompted outrage among English teachers, who were in the vanguard of the boycott of the standard attainment tasks a decade ago.

> (Dean and Henry 2001, in *TES* 27 April 2001)

They are not, and never were intended to be, a checklist to be compulsorily learned by

Key Stage 3 pupils. But, like the collection of commonly misspelt words on pages 46 and 47 of the *Framework*, they were suggested as areas of spelling most likely to present problems for some pupils, to which teachers might like to pay attention. In the light of the whole Strategy, cooler consideration should reassure teachers that they have been given a most practical resource, and their pupils should benefit from this level of detailed teaching.

Spelling

The area of 'new knowledge' secondary teachers appear to be least confident about in their preparation for the Key Stage 3 Strategy is the 'phonemic awareness' expected of them, as a strategy to enable the teaching of spelling. Objectives blithely requiring:

1. correct vowel choices, including: vowels with common alternative spellings, e.g. ay, ai, a-e; unstressed vowels; the influence of vowels on other letters, e.g. *doubling consonants, softening c;*

(DfEE 2001a)

as a topic that 'pupils should revise, consolidate and secure' has caused some departments to quake! Surely, some English teachers have suggested, pupils should have encountered teaching of this sort long before secondary school. The answer is that most pupils are *now* (i.e. since the beginning of the Literacy Strategy in 1998) systematically being taught a phonemic programme in their infant and junior literacy hours, but it was not always the case for all. Subsequently, a large proportion of pupils in the early years of secondary education have not been supplied with the sort of background that might enable them to employ that knowledge easily in their spelling strategies.

When pupils are making choices about their spellings they have to be aware that there are many alternative ways of making the same sound. Examples of the long 'a' sound will be sufficient to make the point:

single 'a' as in able/nation
'ai' as in maid/paid
'aigh' as in straight
'ay' as in may/away
the split digraph 'a-e' as in late/kale
'eigh' as in sleigh/neighbour
'ei' as in vein/rein
'ey' as in they

It is helpful for the learner to have an idea of the possible combinations of letters, and then to use sight memory, contextual application and analogy to make the final choice. This is dealt with in the next section.

Teachers have been helped enormously by the publication of the *Year 7 Spelling Bank* (DfEE 2001c), supplied free to all schools during the training in the summer term 2001. This excellent resource deserves close and careful study by departments. It has been thoroughly written and is presented in a most helpful manner. English staff will also probably learn something new about certain words and word groups (the booklet provides superb groups of spelling patterns). Secondary teachers may not be aware of the equally useful Key Stage 2 Spelling Bank (DfEE 1999b). The likelihood of Year 7 pupils having covered all of the material in the Year 6 booklet is small, yet it would provide a good overlap with some sections they might already have encountered. Secondary teachers should be prepared to plan word level work from both publications.

While most spelling work will probably take place within the 'starter session' of lessons (see Chapter 3) and should be planned over a period of time, good teachers will also conduct 'spelling review sessions', or something similar on a regular basis. Pupils will need opportunities to check their own habitual spelling problems, and address them to bring about improvement. Young people will only ever make worthwhile progress as spellers if they are enabled to take proper responsibility for their own development, and gain insights into areas requiring development. They will need to put a range of strategies into action, and possibly be tested on the specific patterns that have previously given them trouble.

The objectives stress such devices as pupils' knowledge and understanding of morphemes (the smallest units of words, not possible to divide further, capable of changing the word's meaning), for example house/house*s*/house*ful*. Pupils will also be expected to engage more obviously with homophones, and become more confident about knowing the technical terms for the separate areas they are learning. Excellent further advice on spelling strategies can be found in the *Literacy Across the Curriculum* training folder (DfEE 2001e), made available to all schools for whole staff training.

Spelling strategies

Teaching spelling has been a less than systematic practice in some English departments. Policies for the teaching of spelling have not always progressed much beyond suggesting how the teachers identify misspelt words, and the sorts of 'corrections' the pupils might have had to perform as a consequence. Some policies might advocate the imposition of spelling tests, comprising lists of common mistakes, or even groups of words with apparently connected spelling patterns. But, there has been little real focus on the methods by which pupils might help themselves to become more skilled, independent and self-regulating spellers.

Spellers need to be able to call on a range of different tactics in order to address their own difficulties. Initially, they should be encouraged to believe that they are good spellers who make occasional mistakes. Creating a positive spelling culture goes a long way in bringing about spelling success for the majority of pupils. In fact, it is usually true that most pupils are reasonable spellers and the majority of mistakes they make are either lapses of concentration, or fall into differently identifiable categories. So, a writer may not have made, for example, 15 mistakes, but may have repeated the same sort of mistake three or four times.

Over the period of the Key Stage, spellers are expected to grow in confidence and become more skilful in a few related strategies:

1. sounding out the phonemes of the required word (always an important starting point, because some pupils have not actually heard the word properly. An example is a pupil who writes 'sumfing' for 'something');
2. sounding out and breaking words into syllables: it can be easier working in parts, rather than tackling the whole word;

3. using onset and rhyme as a means of applying analogy: if pupils can spell 'cat', they should easily be able to cope with 'fat', 'bat', 'sat', 'mat', 'hat', 'tat', 'rat' etc., as the word comprises the rhyme 'at', preceded by different consonant onsets;

4. draw on analogies to known words, roots, derivations, word families, e.g. beauty, beautiful, beauteous, beautician etc.;

5. use mnemonics, 'sound spellings' and words within words for tricky and awkward words, to ensure that they will be remembered, e.g. *Big Elephants Can't Always Use Small Exits* to yield 'because'; saying clearly aloud the three parts of Wed/nes/day (known as 'sound spelling'); or 'I am' in parl*iam*ent;

6. departments should adopt a Study – Say – Cover – Write – Check – Learn approach, to aid all spellers. This is a development on the 'Look – Cover – Write – Check' method that was once regularly practised, but is now considered less effective than its successor, in that it required the speller only 'to look'. The more modern version asks the learner to actively consider ways of tackling the word in the 'Study' element.

Underpinning all spelling growth and development for classes of pupils should also be a strong insistence on pupil self-monitoring and review. Pupils need to identify the sorts of words commonly misspelt in their work, set them alongside other words that work in the same way (or adopt a learning strategy, such as the one described in point 6 above) and learn the correct versions. Spelling will never be improved by pupils learning random lists of words (no speller's needs can be the same as the other pupils in the class), but they can make progress by being regularly tested on their own identified problems. Indeed, a personal spelling target-setting activity ought to involve collecting samples of their own difficulties, and resolving to sort them out within a specified, agreed time.

Every part of the above section articulating purposeful ways to tackle problems with spelling should be seen as a collaborative approach, which not only involves the whole staff, but is known to other adults, such as the learning support assistants. Pupils learning spelling within that shared culture should pay closer attention to that level of consistent support, and stand to gain considerably from it.

Vocabulary

These objectives are less well developed than those suggesting ways of helping pupils to become more successful spellers. Some of the objectives might have more to do with sentence level learning than with word level activities, for example:

Year 7 Vocabulary
To continue developing their vocabulary, pupils should be able to:
    20. expand the range of link words and phrases used to signpost texts, including links of time (*then, later, meanwhile*) and cause (*so, because, since*);

Year 8 Vocabulary
    10. extend the range of prepositions and connectives used to indicate purpose, e.g. *in order to, so that*, or express reservations, e.g. *although, unless, if;*
(DfEE 2001a: 23, 27)

The objectives also include much vocabulary to be learned about grammatical and linguistic devices and word classes. Pupils are expected to know 'and understand' the metalangue, including 'prepositions, auxiliary verb' (Year 7); 'word class', 'noun phrase', 'subordinate clause', 'syntax', 'conditional' (Year 8). The rather random nature of these objectives suggests that the compilers of the *Framework* were desperately insisting that pupils should be undertaking grammatically based lessons or activities, come what may. They remind some of us of the original primary Literacy Strategy *Framework for Teaching* (DfEE 1998), which was actually published the wrong way round! So keen were its compilers to ensure that phonics work was included in many literacy hours, that they placed the word level column, containing the phonics objectives, on the left hand side of the page thereby suggesting it had precedence over text level considerations.

More realistic are the suggested activities around the following sorts of morphological objective:

Year 8 Vocabulary
7. review and develop their ability to:
(a) recognise the links between words related by word families and roots;
(b) work out the meaning of unknown words using context, syntax, etymology, morphology and other factors;
(c) understand and explain exactly what words mean in particular contexts;

(DfEE 2001a: 27)

What these objectives are really asking of teachers in their future planning is to give priority to making meaning. Pupils should become confident and clearer in their ability to know how language is working, and how the subtleties and nuances of meanings are being conveyed through those linguistic choices.

Finally, in this section, it is necessary to reiterate that unless pupils are subjected to constant reminders about how words are working in different contexts and different subjects – sometimes the same words meaning different things in different circumstances – then their learning will be less developed. These objectives have to be made known to all teachers, and all teachers asked to include them in their planning, teaching, discussion with pupils and general expectations.

Sentence level objectives

'Grammar is back' might be the headline accompanying the announcement of the introduction of the sentence level objectives. However, this is not the grammar most adults would remember from their own schooldays. Unlike the concentration on 'parts of speech' (now known, more accurately, as 'word classes'), and unbending Latinate rules that once predominated in grammar lessons, the modern learning programme is concerned with the way writers convey meaning. A few English teachers will probably have to learn some of the terminology and how to apply the grammatical features themselves, as a large proportion of the current English teacher force have only a limited background in even simple linguistics. This deficit should not be seen as a drawback; it could indeed be an advantage. Teachers could use this opportunity to model learning methods in grammar and sentence level skills. Because they might not be certain of particular facts, they could effectively demonstrate to their classes how to find out what they need to discover, and how to test their knowledge by using their theories in real textual contexts.

Sentence construction and punctuation

Pupils will need to be familiarised with phrases and clauses in this area of their work. Much of this learning follows directly from the *Grammar for Writing* (DfEE 2000) exercises pupils may well have experienced in their Year 6 lessons. The central focus of the objectives in this section is clearly on pupils taking control of sentence structures, and adding as much variety as possible.

Year 7 Pupils should be taught to:
1. extend their use and control of complex sentences . . .
3. use punctuation to clarify meaning, particularly at the boundaries between sentences and clauses;
4. keep tense usage consistent, and manage changes of tense so that meaning is clear;

Year 8
1. combine clauses into complex sentences . . .
2. explore the impact of a variety of sentence structures . . .
3. make good use of a range of punctuation, including colons and semi-colons;

Year 9
1. review and develop the meaning, clarity, organisation and impact of complex sentences in their own writing;

In recent years the QCA has systematically analysed pupils' writing in tests at the end of Key Stages 2 and 3, and these objectives attempt to address the sorts of sentence-related mistakes and pitfalls that have been identified as the major characteristics of weaker writers in that process.

The assumption behind these objectives is that pupils are already familiar with the different structures of simple, compound and complex sentences. They will be unable to 'recognise and use' subordinate clauses unless they know how complex sentences are formed. This is the sort of revision and simple development possible to plan and practise in the starter session. Pupils might be given three simple sentences, for example:

Terry left the house. He was really upset. He worried about what he had said.

They might then be asked to transform these into one sentence, using the correct punctuation:

As Terry, who was really upset, left the house, he worried about what he had said.

or

Worrying about what he had said, Terry, who was really upset, left the house.

or

Terry left the house, really upset, worried about what he had said.

A simple exercise of this nature, practised for a few minutes each day, in a focused starter session will have fulfilled Year 7 Sentence Level (SL) objectives 1 and 3. A great many young people have difficulty in maintaining careful control of simple sentences in Key Stage 3; this programme is designed to help them construct and control more sophisticated and condensed ideas. The outcomes of this improvement should not only lead to more interesting writing, but also maturer thinking skills.

It is also possible to see progression expected through the three years of the Key Stage (and the development from work that should have been undertaken in the primary Strategy). According to the *Framework*, pupils in Year 7 will be expected to '5. use the active or passive voice to suit purpose'. Secondary pupils should have already encountered this learning in Year 6 term 1: '3. to note and discuss how changes from active to passive affect the word order and sense of a sentence'. In Year 9, teachers should be more prepared to contextualise this learning effectively in the activities supporting the objective: '3. write with differing degrees of formality, relating vocabulary and grammar to context, e.g. *using the active or passive voice*'. Unlike much of the random selection of grammatical work once included in a rather haphazard and occasional basis in secondary English lessons, the Key Stage 3 English *Framework* offers a staged approach to linguistic understanding.

The National Literacy Strategy central team, however, do not expect teachers to introduce this level of grammatical insight into their classrooms without support. A very helpful handbook, the *Year 7 Sentence Level Bank* (DfEE 2001d) has been made available to schools. Once again, a supporting booklet should enable even the least confident teachers of grammar to have a clearer idea about the relevant objectives, with suggestions for application in lessons. The booklet also explores in detail the conventions of different non-fiction text types, which could be unfamiliar to secondary English teachers. Particularly useful in this area of linguistic understanding is the comparison between speaking and writing. As with the *Year 7 Spelling Bank* (DfEE 2001c), the booklet is thankfully not set out in lessons, but follows a patterned set of criteria and headings, delineating the principles and conventions of the aspect of language being described and offering examples in writing.

Teachers of Key Stage 3 pupils, however, need to be aware that for the first year or two of the secondary Strategy their pupils may not be as fully prepared as the primary *Framework* would seem to suggest. Primary teachers also had much to learn about teaching grammatical material, and they did not plan those objectives systematically into their work for the first two years of the Literacy Strategy. Since the publication of *Grammar for Writing* (DfEE 2000), primary teachers have been given greater security in this area, and have received some powerful suggestions and examples of suitable work.

Not quite fulfilling the Year 7 Sentence Level objective 2 ('expand nouns and noun phrases, e.g. *by using a prepositional phrase*'), but contributing to its understanding is the following idea. Ask your pupils to begin collecting and considering fiction titles. They will discover just how many are nouns, or noun phrases, for example: *All Quiet on the Western Front; Our Mutual Friend; The Golden Bough; The Sword in the Stone; Tess of the D'Urbervilles; The History Man; The Turn of the Screw; Midnight's Children; Northern Lights; Notes from Underground; Wuthering Heights; Pig-Heart Boy; The Flower King; A Midsummer Night's Dream; The Comedy of Errors; A Handful of Dust; The Sound of Thunder; The Railway Children,* etc. Ask your pupils to find the verbs in them. Then collect some non-fiction titles, and repeat the same analysis. Having studied them, pupils will never look at text titles in the same way again!

Paragraphing and cohesion

This section, traced through the objectives of all three years, speaks for itself. Because there is so much emphasis in the first section on the sentence level objectives, then it is quite reasonable that the next section should be on the structuring and cohesion of sentences in paragraphs. The Year 7 objectives are straightforward requirements about the nature of paragraphing: linked ideas; topic sentences; organisation of material and paragraph cohesion. The expectations in Years 8 and 9 are about developing that knowledge in more mature ways. This material is what most good English teachers have been tackling and demonstrating in their classrooms for years. It will present few difficulties to the experienced and inexperienced. If, however, anyone is in any doubt about the necessary issues to include, the essential starting points for this work are available in the *Year 7 Sentence Level Bank* (DfEE 2001d).

Stylistic conventions of non-fiction

One of the significant areas of development in primary schools during the years since the Strategy was introduced nationally in 1998 has been the study of non-fiction texts. Before 1998 it was difficult to find much, if any, teaching and learning about such texts taking place. Teachers used them in research and topic work, and often to support learning in science, the humanities, technology and other subjects. But their characteristics were not explored and pupils knew little about them and how they worked, when they moved into the essentially non-fiction based curriculum of the secondary school.

It ought, however, to be recorded that most teachers of subjects in the secondary school are *also* unaware of the contents, dynamics and purposeful structuring of non-fiction texts. 'Information' (or 'non-chronological report'), 'recount', 'explanation', 'instructions', 'persuasion' and 'discursive' text types have been selected for further development in the secondary school, because these were the areas of non-fiction studied throughout Key Stages 1 and 2, and they ought to be thoroughly familiar to all incoming Year 7 pupils. In their new secondary schools these pupils should 'revise' what they know about these types of text, and the 'conventions of non-fiction' suggest themselves as activities to be planned and undertaken early in the school year.

As has been argued earlier in this book, these objectives cannot solely be the responsibility of the English teachers. In the *Literacy Across the Curriculum* training folder (DfEE 2001e), written to introduce shared literacy issues to all teachers in the schools, is a large module on 'Writing non-fiction'. This contains detailed references to all six text types mentioned in the previous paragraph (familiar to all recent ex-primary pupils), and two additional types – 'analysis', including essay writing, and 'evaluation' – which are more characteristic of secondary school writing practices. The overlap of the *Framework* and the literacy training folder is clear. English teachers can help pupils bring their knowledge from primary school literacy lessons into the secondary school, and even help exemplify the ways those texts work, but the ultimate development and responsibility for the fullest teaching and dissemination of the non-fiction text types rests with all staff.

Through Years 7, 8 and 9 pupils are expected to explore the use and conventions, and apply the text types appropriately, to become wholly accustomed to their employment in a variety of contexts, formal and informal.

Standard English and language variation

This section, across all three Years of Key Stage 3, is intended to help pupils pay much closer attention to the written system of language, differentiating it quite clearly from the spoken system.

> I talk talking. I write writing. I do not talk writing, and I do not write talking, except in the preliminary stages. Historically, the written language was felt to be the model for the spoken ... Now they are seen as different, each with its own integrity, though related.
>
> (Wilkinson 1986)

In earlier versions of official English documentation it would have been common to see these matters made more of, and highlighted at a much earlier stage. The *Framework*, more sensibly and realistically, makes them yet another grammatical consideration, without over-emphasising their importance.

Nevertheless, considerable numbers of young people leave school without realising that the act of writing necessitates calling on a huge set of processes, about which many decisions have to be made. Writing is such a difficult activity; to be purposeful, directed, controlled and successful the brain has to be fully engaged. Pupils becoming increasingly reflective of their literacy development have to be enabled to articulate clearly what they are undertaking as they write (see the list of writers' qualities on page 78). This section should provide the objectives on which that area of learning can be more specifically built.

3 The four part English lesson structure

When the Key Stage 3 Strategy was first proposed, a collective shiver went down the backs of English teachers, who feared that they might have to adopt the Literacy Hour, such a strong feature of the primary Literacy Strategy. Indeed, for some of those who misunderstood its real intentions, or who deliberately misrepresented it, the Literacy Hour *was* the primary Literacy Strategy. Practical considerations, however, meant that the Hour was not to be the central recommended model of organisation in secondary schools.

The first obstacle raised about that particular time allocation is that many secondary schools do not timetable lessons of one hour. Some do allocate that length of time per lesson, but others have lesson periods ranging from 30 to 90 minutes. So, quite realistically, the *Framework* offers the following advice:

> Because schools must work within different time constraints, there is no single structure for lessons using the Framework. The structure of the lesson *must serve the objectives.*
>
> (DfEE 2001a: 17, my emphasis)

and then:

> The following lesson structure *is recommended to teachers using the Framework, but it is not intended to be a straitjacket. Teachers should adapt it to suit the objectives in hand and the length of the school lesson.*
> 1. Short lesson starter activity (e.g. spelling, vocabulary) lasting 10–15 minutes
> 2. Introduce the main teaching points (e.g. teacher exposition or questioning)
> 3. Develop the main teaching points (e.g. through group activity)
> 4. Plenary to draw out the learning (e.g. through feedback and presentation), lasting 5–10 minutes.
>
> (DfEE 2001a: 17, my emphasis)

The message is unambiguous. Not a single English department *has* to adopt the four part lesson. No department has to adopt the four part lesson for even some of the time. Circumstances of timing, learning objectives, particular activities or resources, amongst others, might cause the structure of any lesson to be reconsidered. Adhering to structural features of the lesson should never be the cause of anxiety or concern for any teacher. But, the four part lesson is recommended advisedly; it is not a whim or passing fad, or the apparatus of external interference! The reasons for its adoption, and some of the ways it might be best used are outlined below.

The lesson starter

One of the least familiar parts of the recommended lesson structure is the 10 to 15 minute starter. To become fully effective it will require some practice – success will not be found overnight – and teachers will need to make appropriate adaptations according to the nature of their English classes.

One reason for its adoption is to get the lesson off to a brisk start. In the pilot classrooms, where first tested, it overwhelmingly had the effect of motivating pupils to arrive on time, and to be prepared to begin work immediately. Many word level objectives can be easily adapted to take place within this part of the lesson, for example Year 7 Word Level (WL) objectives 1 to 6, 8 to 12 can be virtually used as described on page 22 of the *Framework*. Most teachers would probably want to wrap the exercises up in more opportunities for learning, but they require little adjustment. The Sentence Level (SL) objectives will usually need more careful attention, particularly in those circumstances where teachers may be wanting to explore instances of unusual or interesting language use in real textual contexts (a way of working with texts I firmly recommend!).

The important point to address is that these objectives should be drawn together by the teaching staff in such a way that they make a substantial and worthwhile 'learning package', effectively contributing to the way that the pupils approach spelling and vocabulary issues in their later development. The starter is *not* to be regarded as a time filler, or in any way subordinate to other parts of the lesson. It has its own legitimate validity; it differs from the rest of the work merely in its timescale.

The publishing market is likely to be awash with books of suggested 'Starter Activities' in the foreseeable future, and the reasonable temptation will be to buy in copies to ease teachers' planning. The advice being offered is not that departments should resist the 'temptation' – far from it – but that when looking through and considering sample copies, English teachers should consider which set of books will support most securely an already agreed learning programme about word level, or spelling, work. The learning programme should determine the manner of resources, not the other way round! Similarly, books containing sentence level exercises should not be merely second-rate substitutes for the once ubiquitous 'grammar worksheets'. To be at all worth while, these sorts of exercise have to encourage pupils to explore language use in real contexts, and allow them to reflect on their findings.

More alert English departments will be looking closely at a most welcome free resource, the *Year 7 Spelling Bank* (DfEE 2001c), supplied by the National Literacy publications department. This excellent resource is a mine of information for teachers about patterns of letters and sounds and relationships between words, many of which are unknown to or previously unconsidered by secondary teachers. This book is a natural development from the equally good Key Stage 2 *Spelling Bank* (DfEE 1999b), much of which is just as suitable for Year 7 pupils. The pages are not set out as ready-made starter activities, but it would not take teachers very long to structure whole sets of starter sessions from the available material.

Here are some suggestions on ways of using the starter session:

- keep the exercise as straightforward as possible, and aim for the quickest possible start, as a long explanation of what pupils are required to do misses the point;

- do not over-plan this part of the lesson, as it will become burdensome and lose its point if it takes up a disproportionate amount of planning and preparation. Alternatively, *enjoy* an occasional brainstorming session with other members of the department to plan the next series;
- build in a level of challenge, but ensure that most pupils enjoy regular success;
- differentiate activities appropriately for more able pupils, to maintain their interest and ensure that they are properly engaged (they might be invited to devise and run some sessions);
- make as many activities as collaborative as possible; pupils should benefit from discussing ideas and having to make genuine decisions;
- make some sessions genuinely investigative and exploratory, with the possibility of more than just 'right or wrong' responses;
- allow some of the more linguistic/grammar-based exercises to give rise to more than one possible outcome or answer, to make the point that not all language knowledge is solidly based and that there can be alternatives;
- stress the longitudinal learning objectives to which each session contributes and try to ensure that the pupils can see the relationship between lessons (they should not be stand-alone);
- attempt some more open-ended exercises occasionally with responses likely to surprise you;
- encourage pupils to continue thinking or researching about the issues raised in this session through the rest of the week;
- build in an element of competition, especially with younger pupils;
- use resources such as A4 or A5 whiteboards and marker pens to enable pupils to record their findings, but rub them out and start again if necessary;
- assign occasional homework time to pupils thinking about/researching possible ideas for the next lesson's starter, so they do not always come to the exercise 'cold'. All pupils should be invited to think about texts they are reading/pieces they are writing as source material for a possible starter session;
- dedicate the occasional 'plenary session' to reflection and summary about word level/sentence level issues raised through a collection of starter lessons;
- keep it quick! No more than 15 minutes should ever be given to this part of the lesson. Its briskness, focus and intensity should be its prime asset.

Not every lesson needs to begin with a starter session. Some schools have lessons, for instance, of 35 minutes with occasional 'double periods'. If some English lessons are only 35 minutes long, then it would be impractical to expect 10–15 minutes to be given to a starter activity. There will also be occasions when a class might visit the library, or the computer room, or want to continue with research begun in a previous lesson, when a starter session would be inappropriate.

The greatest benefit of the starter session is to bring important matters of word, spelling, vocabulary and grammar to the attention of pupils in a regular, but brisk, manner. We want our students to begin 'noticing' aspects of the language at work; to consider why it has been employed in that manner in that particular context, and to be able to incorporate that knowledge in subsequent textual engagements. It is not necessary to relate the starter to the rest of the English lesson, although if that relationship is possible then stress it! Wherever possible, remind pupils of instances of language use they might have encountered in starter sessions when those examples are seen at work in subsequent reading, writing or speaking activities. Pupils should be positively urged to say aloud and comment on every instance they recognise, within reason of course.

The starter sessions will have proved their worth where a department has identified the precise areas of learning it should be ensuring across a term, or possibly a year or even the whole Key Stage, and can then monitor those improvements. That sort of quality medium- or long-term planning is exactly what the Strategy is designed to bring about.

The main sections of most English lessons

It is only possible to offer the broadest advice about this part of the lesson, as circumstances will be so variable from class to class, lesson to lesson, and teacher to teacher. On page 16 of the *Framework* are lists of aspirations to do with teaching and learning in English lessons:

> Schools are diverse, but the principles of teaching and learning on which the current pilot is founded are universal and well established in research and practice.
> The Key Stage 3 National Strategy promotes **teaching** that is:
>
> - informed by clear, challenging and progressive objectives
> - direct and explicit
> - highly interactive
> - inspiring and motivating
> - varied in style and distinguished by a fast pace and strong focus
> - well-pitched to pupils' needs
> - inclusive and ambitious
>
> (DfEE 2001a)

Most of these highly desirable ways of working can be made more possible by using the main body of the English lesson in an effective and directed manner. (No book can bring about an inspiring and motivating lesson!) Some suggestions are set out below.

- *informed by clear, challenging and progressive objectives*

Lessons containing these features will depend on how well the long term, medium term and short term planning arrangements relate to each other, through the efforts of the whole department (see Chapter 7). Through their interaction with pupils in lessons, all English departments want those young people to read, write, speak and listen more successfully and confidently. The most effective planning will be that which identifies the most appropriate stages and steps to bring about learning – in what George Keith, the linguist, calls 'the four gerunds of English' – in broad, more distinct and very detailed terms. While the actual learning that pupils might achieve in an English lesson can never be fully planned for or quantified, all departments should be moving towards a position where they have, at least, begun to describe the sorts of desired outcomes of lessons, as the starting point for tracking progression and reasonable development.

● *direct and explicit*

There is much to learn about texts through directed close study of language and meaning, and a good deal of that learning has the potential to be fascinating and worth while for pupils of all abilities. 'Direct and explicit' teaching does not mean that teachers adopt a didactic stance, with all the connotations of 'chalk and talk'; those methods challenged and changed by English teachers, particularly, in the late 1960s and 1970s. It means demonstrating openly and explicitly to pupils the sorts of issues or interests texts can excite, how to look out for them, or construct them in their own writing; and how to gain greater confidence to enable better independent encounters with them.

So, for instance, using an extract, typical of the whole text for the teaching of reading, the teacher will show the whole class how to put the sorts of questions that would allow them to make greater sense of its possible meanings. As a result, pupils should become better acquainted with the possible repertoire of approaches, and readier to apply such strategies for themselves when coming across similar, but different, material. Through this manner of teaching known as 'shared reading' or 'shared writing', teachers would be explicitly going through a role play exercise, as if thinking aloud about reading and writing processes often taken for granted. (See 'Shared reading and shared writing' section on pages 44–6.)

Every time that teachers introduce a new genre, text type or form of text to their pupils, they are being asked to spend 15–20 minutes or so pointing out the best ways to apply themselves to discovering the possible range of meanings available, and to explain the evidence leading to those discoveries. Over time, their pupils are expected to become accustomed to using similar questions, or planning and setting up their own writing (or speaking tasks) in more structured and systematic ways.

● *highly interactive*

Most English lessons are already characterised by much talk, discussion and interaction between pupils and teachers, and pupils working together. From my own observations across the curriculum, it is certainly true that more of those interactions take place in English than in most other subjects in secondary schools. English teachers are being asked, however, to go one stage further.

Obviously, the starter session recommended at the beginning of lessons should be the first highly interactive, participative activity pupils become used to. But, while the teacher might be 'demonstrating' how to apply the 'shared reading' or 'shared writing' principles to the texts being studied, pupils should be encouraged to join in and offer suggestions for the possible ways forward (teachers should be prepared in such sessions to receive occasional suggestions they might not have anticipated for themselves!). In the independent learning and consolidation part of the lesson, while the teacher is engaged with smaller groups, the other pupils should be collaboratively engaged; sharing ideas, possible insights and their new textual knowledge. Finally, pupils are expected to evaluate the manner, style and extent of their learning in the plenary, reflective part of the lesson. They should become better listeners to each other through this process.

● *inspiring and motivating*

'Interactive', in this context, also means being busy and involved with textual material. English lesson time should not be used for dull, limited, closed exercises. Text should be material with which pupils are constantly making and remaking relationships. They might enjoy the content of published text, be stirred by it, discover (or bring about in their own writing) lively effects and devices employed by the author, or they might possibly despise and be annoyed by what they are exploring or devising. But they should be expected to, and helped to, make some form of genuine connection with it.

● *varied in style and distinguished by a fast pace and strong focus*

This aspiration grows from the previous one. English lessons, in their four part recommended structure, already contain different styles of working: the brisk, lively starter activity, followed by demonstration and then pupil consolidation, and usually concluded with some form of evaluation. Each of these sections, however, is also capable of being framed in a variety of ways on different occasions.

Most English teachers plan carefully to ensure that their pupils regularly experience different sorts of lessons. Giving greater attention to learning objectives in their work should also stimulate English staff to consider a broader assortment of classroom activities, capable of supporting and enhancing those objectives. Pupils should become accustomed to:

text-marking
text comparison
exercises in close scrutiny
intensive 'drafting' and redrafting on small-scale pieces
experimentation
collaborative evaluation of each other's work
pattern making
speculation and question raising

all more attractive and engaging alternatives to comprehension exercises, characters' diaries, and the interminable unfocused 'Kraznir-type' narratives, to name but a few of the random examples from exhausted Key Stage 3 programmes still seen in some schools.

Some secondary English teachers, acquainting themselves with the primary Literacy Strategy by visiting the lessons of their colleagues teaching Year 5 and 6 classes, have been genuinely astonished with the pace of those encounters. Pupils, fully used to the routines of the lesson, move through the different sections of the Hour with the minimum of fuss, and achieve a great deal of work in the given time. Because so many pupils enjoy their lessons they are also prepared to contribute positively to them, and the majority of the class will take a full part in the proceedings. The secondary school teachers who participated in the pilot Strategy during 2000/2001, reported that their lessons 'speeded up', with more being achieved as a result. A clearer focus on the learning objectives can play a significant part in helping pupils have greater confidence in knowing what they are expected to accomplish, as well as giving the impression of time used effectively.

● *well-pitched to pupils' needs*

It would be difficult to find anybody disagreeing with this ambition. One of the identified shortcomings of the Key Stage 3 programme making the establishment of the Strategy necessary was the imposition of an English curriculum in Year 7 that failed to pick up pupils from the point their learning had reached in primary school. The evidence of bored Year 7 pupils, being expected to read texts far simpler than those already studied in Year 5, or required to write less demanding pieces of work than had been undertaken in Year 6, was strongly convincing and observed in schools nationally. Primary teachers had complained for years that not only were secondary English colleagues failing to acknowledge and act on the results of the Key Stage 2 tests (with some justification, as it happened), but their liaison meetings often left them with the impression that primary English lessons were regarded as poor preparation for the 'rigours' of Key Stage 3. This situation, not wholly the fault of secondary English teachers, was becoming seriously worrying and had to be addressed. The relationship of the primary and secondary *Frameworks* offers a huge opportunity for teachers from the consecutive phases of education to communicate more effectively and purposefully with each other.

Some features of the two *Frameworks* deliberately overlap. The sentence level work in Year 6 Term 3 of the primary *Framework* Strategy (DfEE 1998) states:

Grammatical awareness
1. to revise the language conventions and grammatical features of the different types of text such as:

- narrative (e.g. stories and novels)
- recounts (e.g. anecdotes, accounts of observations, experiences)
- instructional texts (e.g. instructions and directions)
- reports (e.g. factual writing, description)
- explanatory texts (how and why)
- persuasive texts (e.g. opinions, promotional literature)
- discursive texts (e.g. balanced arguments)

(DfEE 1998: 54)

The Year 7 Sentence Level objectives included in the Key Stage 3 *Framework* (DfEE 2001a) under the subheading 'Stylistic conventions of non-fiction', state:

13. revise the stylistic conventions of the main types of non-fiction:

(a) *Information*, which maintains the use of the present tense and the third person, organises and links information clearly, incorporates examples;
(b) *Recount*, which maintains the use of the past tense, clear chronology and temporal connectives;
(c) *Explanation*, which maintains the use of the present tense and impersonal voice, and links points clearly;
(d) *Instructions*, which are helpfully sequenced and signposted, deploy imperative verbs and provide clear guidance;
(e) *Persuasion*, which emphasises key points and articulates logical links in the argument;
(f) *Discursive writing*, which signposts the organisation of contrasting points and clarifies the viewpoint.

(DfEE 2001a: 23)

Without making too much of the constant references to 'revision' of the linguistic features, these obviously related objectives have to be taken seriously by Year 7 teachers, and the overlaps taken into account in any planning. If they are to bring about a smoother transition for those youngsters from the primary to the secondary phase, secondary English departments should have more than a passing acquaintance with the whole Year 6 English/literacy programme, as well as the recommended objectives for their own pupils.

'Well-pitched to pupils' needs' has another meaning too. The Key Stage 3 English strand learning objectives are intended for all pupils. It is not a programme for those pupils who have experienced previous difficulties with their language/literacy studies as they have moved through the educational system (although there are some special features for such pupils). All pupils, even the most confident and able, are expected to benefit from the introduction of the Strategy. This broad overview contains some important implications, particularly in relation to the provision of effectively differentiated teaching programmes. A 'one size fits all' model of English planning will not be sufficient or adequate; every department has to recognise the range of abilities contained in each year group and address their needs carefully by constructing appropriately demanding learning programmes for all.

There is absolutely no need to place pupils into ability 'sets' as a result of the introduction of the English strand of the Key Stage 3 Strategy. In many respects, to split pupils of differing abilities into separate teaching groups for English/literacy/ language studies is a mistaken approach. Pupils learn language, and how to use language more effectively, in many different circumstances. The learning of language capability is not regarded as a 'linear' development in contemporary thinking; it is not an incremental, staged process. While English teachers have to make necessary decisions about those particular elements of language/literacy/literary learning they regard as essential for the many learning and social contexts their pupils are likely to encounter, much of that learning – invaluable as it is – is incidental and unplanned. Pupils are not just different in terms of ability; they have gender differences, differences in backgrounds, linguistic experiences and differences of maturity. 'Differentiation', if it is to be meaningful, should address all these aspects of each pupil: 'A simple definition might be "recognising differences between learners and the planned use of these differences to maximise their learning"' (Daw 1995). While it is obvious that pupils with less language knowledge or confidence can often benefit from hearing and seeing their more linguistically adept peers in action, the process is in fact reciprocal. Utterances and insights made by the weaker pupils can also exercise the capacity to stir and interest those regarded as more capable.

Because English – whether in its language, literacy or literary manifestation – can never be regarded as a 'body of knowledge' to be transmitted from teacher to pupil, it should not be a subject at Key Stage 3 where pupils are divided for reasons of ability. Pupils who may already have lower language horizons than other members of their academic year should not be condemned to at least five more years of limited opportunities. They need and deserve the richest language learning possible if they are to make any sort of progress against their already heavy odds.

● *inclusive and ambitious*
Pupils of all abilities and capabilities are intended to benefit from the English strand of the Key Stage 3 Strategy. It is simply not possible to have seen all the potential

meanings to be discovered in texts, raised all the available questions about them, or ever to compose a piece of writing that cannot be improved in some respect. Certainly, a large proportion of pupils will be given support through these studies to become more confident language users in fairly straightforward, not to say commonplace situations, although good teachers will have higher aspirations for them. But our secondary schools should also be properly providing for some 10–15 per cent of pupils whose ability is well above the average (possibly even up to 25 per cent, if the numbers of pupils currently achieving Level 5+ in English at the end of Key Stage 2 is any sort of realistic guide). These pupils, along with those with Special Educational Needs (SEN), those with disabilities and those learning English as an Additional Language (EAL) are mentioned and given extra consideration specifically in the Key Stage 3 *Framework* (DfEE 2001a), on pages 57–72. This section needs careful attention by all English departments; it is very easy in a busy and demanding schedule to focus attention completely on the ten pages listing the recommended learning objectives. (See Chapter 8 for further discussion.)

'Targets' have become a cliché in this age. The Labour government has forced 'targets' on all manner of public services and organisations, even setting up targets for reducing the death rates of certain hospitals. Yet, hidden within this rather brutal and blunt manner of addressing some areas of public life, where improvement has been deemed necessary and possible, are devices for better and efficient focusing of attention on data, and how to address the evidence the data provide. Primary teachers, subject to 'target-setting' procedures in their schools, have begun to ask more worthwhile questions about the ways their pupils learn, and the potential they show for eventual success, in an effort to support the 'raising of standards' (i.e. the numbers of pupils reaching agreed numerical levels in tests). This more directed form of investigation has led to better support programmes being constructed for groups and individuals in large numbers of schools. Rather than being satisfied with broad, unhelpful targets, such as certain percentages of a whole year achieving a given goal, many schools have become more careful about investigating these smaller units contributing to the school's overall percentage figure: each individual pupil. In this way, a number of head teachers have been able to suggest, realistically, that with the appropriate and necessary degrees of support, the correct resources and establishment of a fully developed literacy culture, more pupils are capable of achieving better results. Considerable numbers of primary teachers who, before the introduction of the Literacy Strategy, were not optimistic about the likely results of many of their pupils have adjusted their predictions upwards, because they have seen the transformational qualities of a genuinely developmental programme.

Larger numbers of young people can do better and achieve more through their language and literacy studies, and their increased success should lead to improved self-esteem, confidence and willingness to attempt other improved outcomes. Teachers need to be asking themselves, at the various levels of ability and capability at which they assess their pupils, which other aspects of the overall programme will be most suitable to sustain that improvement.

An 'ambitious' attitude is not the sole province of the English teacher, in this context. If pupils are to make the sorts of progress being promoted as possible, by government ministers, the National Literacy Strategy, LEA staff and others, then they cannot bring about those outcomes without the help and cooperation of their colleagues in other subject departments. It will be possible for pupils to make quite strong gains in the sorts of learning promoted by English lessons, but that development can only really be consolidated where attention to linguistic and literacy issues is being actively reinforced and consolidated in all the complementary areas of learning provided by the school. Without the active interest and long-term support of the other teachers, the learning and progress brought about as a result of English lessons will not be seen at its fullest. If teachers of science, history and technology, for example, want their pupils to read and write more successfully, and use talk to enhance their learning, then these ambitions will be reflected in the even greater improved performance of pupils in English. As in many walks of life, it is difficult to realise these sorts of ambition in isolation.

Shared reading and shared writing

The National Literacy Strategy has already developed ways of working more effectively . . . through the use of:

- shared reading and writing – in which the teacher demonstrates and models the process of comprehension or composition with the whole class;
- guided reading and writing – in which the teacher dedicates substantial time in the lesson to support and stretch a particular group;

(DfEE 2001a: 17)

Teachers already use shared reading and shared writing techniques in their English lessons; they have been employed, without comment or drawing attention to themselves, for years. In the changed lesson structure, however, these teaching methods should be given more attention, be very deliberately practised and explicitly noticed by all the participants.

For too long there has been an assumption in considerable numbers of English classrooms that pupils naturally know how to read texts placed in front of them. Of course, teachers have taken care to ensure that the material is usually manageable and accessible, but they have not often paused to think about some of the possible ways of making engagement with the text the pupil might be employing. Reading is a hugely complex process, involving very many ways of making meaning, which change according to the context. 'Shared reading' used effectively means that the teacher has given attention to each of the many strands of the process, has taken nothing for granted, and will demonstrate clearly to the class how to make the fullest engagement(s) with the text(s) under consideration by highlighting the individual parts.

Shared reading should be approached as if the teacher is conducting a role-play situation. All the hidden, usually silent, mental processes that are normally intrinsic and unremarked by experienced readers should be brought to the surface and made obvious in this process. So, as well as demonstrating how to practise and improve a particular learning objective (take, for example, the Year 7 Text Level Reading for meaning objectives, which requires pupils to '**9.** distinguish between the views of the writer and those expressed by others in the text, e.g. *the narrator, quoted experts, characters*'), the teacher is also practising, and helping the pupils to adopt a similar approach, and learning how to make an actual engagement with the text in the first place. The teacher takes the pupils through all the very evident stages, speaking out loud and sharing those moments at all points, as if from the view of the learner. This sort of discourse might proceed in the following manner:

> Teacher: 'Now, I have been asked to look out for . . . I have been informed that this text is a good example of . . . My teacher has suggested that I look at pages . . . , because there are some instances of . . . I have found the pages, and immediately I should be looking for . . . I could ask myself, at this point, "how long are the sentences? which word, or sort of word keeps reoccurring? what do I notice about the way this group of words has been put together?" So, from this evidence, I am beginning to think that . . . ', etc.

Pupils not only see their teachers dealing with texts, but they hear and have an excellent chance to see rehearsed the thought processes of a more experienced practitioner, and begin to acquire a repertoire of 'skills of engagement' for themselves. This form of learning owes much to the research work of the Russian psychologist, Vygotsky.

> In the child's development . . . imitation and instruction play a major role. They bring out the specifically human qualities of the mind and lead the child to new developmental levels . . . What the child can do in cooperation today he can do alone tomorrow. Therefore the only good kind of instruction is that which marches ahead of development and leads it; it must be aimed not so much at the ripe as the ripening functions.

> (Vygotsky 1986)

Obviously, this would be a rather boring and self-indulgent activity if it is not clearly to do with the actual learning needs of the pupils, and – more importantly – if it does not actively involve them in explaining what is taking place and inviting their participation. As they become accustomed to the teacher working in this way, so the pupils begin to offer suggestions about what to do. They help to raise actual questions, or move into the position of guiding the teacher through a set of stages. They are expected to step into the role play, and become real actors in a real learning situation. It is not a state of affairs that all teachers will immediately feel comfortable conducting, but their colleagues in Key Stages 1 and 2 soon began to adapt their practice in this manner, and discovered how effective it can be as a learning device.

'Shared writing' lends itself even more readily to pupil participation. Again, the teacher gives considerable attention to the different decisions possible to be made, as a piece of text is constructed before the eyes of the class. (Indeed, one of the central features pupils would always be expected to note in the process of writing is just how many decisions there are to make!) From the outset, the teacher will place exaggerated emphasis on the *purpose* of the writing, calling on the assistance of the class to offer suggestions about the likely structural and grammatical devices necessary to support that purpose. Teachers will take opportunities to practise drafting skills, attempting alternative lines, or longer passages, to show how various possibilities are always available to the writer. Pupils would be expected to practise deciding which versions of the text best suited their intentions, and justifying those decisions. Teachers writing in this manner offer a powerful model for their pupils, who realise more obviously the conscious and deliberate 'constructedness' of textual composition. As a result of this 'modelling' pupils are expected to approach their own writing tasks similarly, by raising the same questions and addressing the same issues.

The most demanding part of employing shared reading and writing techniques with any class is being able to involve and motivate pupils of different abilities. Some pupils might well have problems actually decoding the text, while others in the room could well be asking a range of complex and searching questions about its possible meanings. This situation should not be seen as an impossible obstacle. Raising expectations of pupils' eventual achievements means always having a clear idea of what they could manage, given suitable support. As Vygotsky claims:

> It remains necessary to determine the lowest threshold at which instruction in, say, arithmetic may begin, since a certain minimal ripeness of functions is required. But we must consider the upper threshold as well; instruction must be orientated toward the future, not the past.

(Vygotsky 1986)

Skilled teachers will attempt to interest pupils at their own level, through asking differentiated questions. Even less confident readers can still have opinions about a text, and comment on certain features of its ways of making meaning, as long as they have some idea of what they are seeking in their scrutiny of the text. Teachers in Key Stage 2 have been surprised by the renewed motivation of certain pupils, particularly boys, who once might have been described as 'struggling readers'. Although their poor decoding skills have limited their involvement in textual encounters in the past, they have improved their personal commitment to their work by being given more focused grounds for probing and shown how to question in better detail. Their decoding has usually improved, as a consequence, too.

Whatever the range of ability in any class, the teacher is still addressing broad learning intentions, relevant to every pupil. Shared reading and shared writing are devices for approaching learning principles required by the whole group. The extent and depth of the learning of individuals, and the ways in which more able pupils might have the capability to apply their new knowledge, are factors that the teacher then has to discover through other means, including 'guided reading' and 'guided writing'. Perhaps one of the differences between the way English was approached before and after the introduction of the Strategy lies in this way of teaching. Before the Strategy a number of learning areas were addressed 'as they came up', possibly resulting from issues arising from a text being read, or problems arising from pupils' writing. Contained within the spirit of the Strategy is an expectation that certain specified learning matters, outlined in the objectives, will be tackled come what may, and the shared reading and shared writing methods are excellent contexts in which to promote that learning style.

Guided reading and guided writing

While shared reading and shared writing are reasonably familiar to most English teachers, the accompanying 'guided' methods for teaching reading and writing are probably new ways of working for most secondary staff. At its simplest, guided reading means the teacher sitting down with a small group of pupils (between six and eight) of similar abilities, giving them undivided attention for a period of some 10–20 minutes. Through discussion and careful, supportive questioning, at an appropriate level for that group of pupils, the teacher is able to ascertain the extent of their insights and understanding about the specific textual features they should be studying.

This, clearly differentiated, manner of working closely alongside pupils enables the teacher to discover much about an individual's level of involvement, and the quality of questions being raised about the meanings of texts, while also allowing the teacher to support and challenge further. English teachers, like their colleagues in all subjects, have regularly 'patrolled' their classrooms, after setting work for their pupils, ensuring that everybody understands the point of the exercise, everybody is 'on task', and reducing any misunderstandings. But there are drawbacks to what the Key Stage 3 *Framework for Teaching English* calls 'unplanned circulation', where the teacher's time is not always put to 'optimum use'. This more focused way of underpinning pupils' learning follows up, almost at individual level, the broader principles offered to the whole class in the 'shared' session. In this interchange teachers should be able to assist their pupils in raising particular sorts of questions about their reading, encouraging and making clearer relationships between separate parts.

A group of less confident readers might be capable of making some progress through their individual textual encounters, while more able classmates are expected to compare different texts, or consider more generalised issues of whole genre study as examples of differentiated study. The teacher, visiting each group in turn systematically over an agreed period of time, is then in a position to move each one forward at an appropriate speed. Such a way of working would be very beneficial for more able pupils, and even those pupils requiring extra support have the opportunity to work independently at a manageable pace. Another strength of this classroom organisation is that reluctant or shy speakers have better opportunities to discuss matters in a 'safer' way, and are likely to feel readier to share ideas with their teachers. Teachers who realise that members of a group have not really understood the main points of the intended learning can revisit the objectives, or spend a little longer cementing more firmly the central issues being explored.

It is, of course, essential that pupils establish good working habits, and accept that they have a responsibility to their own learning development before this method can be successfully adopted. They have to be ready to work cooperatively, unsupervised, for longish periods of time, because the teacher is committed to a specific group in another part of the room. Their turn will come, but it can only be worth while, enjoying the teacher's full attention, if there are no distractions from other groups. The teacher of a less able class might elect to spend no more than ten minutes or so with any group, thus ensuring regular contact with everybody, and keeping the class more consistently on task.

Guided sessions make efficient use of teacher time when pupils are working independently, and pupils appreciate the access that guided sessions give them to the teacher. Teachers are encouraged to schedule regular opportunities to visit each group in the class for focused time of this sort.

(DfEE 2001a: 18)

Guided reading is one of the most effective ways of teaching reading for secondary pupils. Used well it is a very powerful tool in assisting pupils to gain the greatest possible meaning from texts. The most helpful way of making the session work well is by having individual copies of the text being studied for everybody in the group, or, if resources are limited, one copy between two readers. The teacher is then able to ask the pupils to look closely at specific areas of the text, even to read them silently as preparation for discussion, and to direct their attention carefully. In this way pupils can be asked to find the evidence from anywhere in the text to support their arguments and assertions, to relate patterns of language or related ideas, or the features of genre and text type independently. They can also be asked to follow carefully if the teacher is reading a particularly notable illustrative passage and the teacher is able to judge how much genuine interaction is taking place. The questions put to the groups should enable them to make real progress during the period of one of these sessions, and teachers might well ask themselves, 'what more do these pupils know about dealing with this sort of text than they did before they started?' If some new ways of approaching texts have been introduced into the shared session, then teachers can use this group context to assess whether the skills that have been taught are actually understood and being put to work.

Teachers can also hear pupils read aloud in these small group situations, to check on their ability to decode and make total sense when confronted with unfamiliar material. This is a much fairer and more supportive way of asking pupils to read aloud, because many are intimidated by being asked to read to a whole class.

Guided writing can be equally cogent in teaching writing. It is also possible to employ it in a variety of ways, depending on the stage of writing being considered. As with guided reading, the teacher works alongside a small group of pupils with similar linguistic abilities. After having established some learning principles in the shared writing session, the class would be divided into groups to practise composing a similar or related piece of their own, or even a collaborative composition in the style of the modelled text. Teachers have a number of different opportunities to support and develop their pupils' skills. They might, for instance, be working with a group preparing to write. The sorts of questions this group would be putting to itself, to identify the writing issues with which it should be engaging, will be different from a group already having completed some of its writing. The former group will be preoccupied with making the early decisions about appropriate text type and related grammatical structures, while the latter collection of pupils will be more concerned with checking through what has been accomplished to ensure that earlier intentions have been complied with, and sense and meaning maintained. In the same vein, a teacher working alongside a group with its written task almost complete, will be encouraging them to apply their critical skills to the finished piece in a quite different way.

Guided writing allows teachers to involve their pupils much more successfully and directly in their own learning, as pupils have to justify and explain choices they have made in more demanding one-to-one situations. The teacher is able to intervene more potently into pupils' work while it is being composed, or even while it is being planned. While one group receives intensive support, the other groups working independently can concentrate on small-scale, manageable outcomes in a short-term collaborative enterprise. Actually beginning the process of writing is a particular problem for less accomplished language users; they experience difficulty in committing themselves to print. Guided writing can offer hesitant pupils ways of setting off in their writing tasks, and is likely to increase their confidence.

Guided writing, like guided reading, allows teachers to work more sensitively with pupils of different abilities concerned in the same sorts of tasks. A less able group could be attempting a short whole text, ensuring that they are including all the characteristic features of a particular text type. Their more able classmates could, at the same time, be endeavouring to write a short, but intensively focused paragraph typical of the writer being used as a model. Indeed, the two extremes of ability could be pursuing the same task, but the level of knowledge and sophistication they are expected to bring to their work is regulated, orchestrated and differentiated by the teacher.

The *Framework for Teaching English* offers the following overview:

Very often, teachers will develop the main objective of a lesson by giving time for pupils to work in groups. This allows the teacher to work intensively with one group on the current objective, or to develop skills taught earlier in reading and writing. Guided sessions support pupils as they apply their new knowledge in context and the teacher is able to give immediate feedback. It may be used, for example, to:

- support a group of weaker readers tackling a common text (e.g. helping them to infer and deduce meanings);
- give feedback on work in progress (e.g. written homework);
- consolidate an objective that has not been well grasped by the group (e.g. revisiting insecure punctuation);
- review personal and group reading (e.g. discussing a text in progress with an able group).

Guided sessions make efficient use of teacher time when pupils are working independently . . .

(DfEE 2001a: 18)

The plenary

Probably the part of the Literacy Hour that has taken the longest time to successfully develop has been the plenary session. The plenary was designed, within the Literacy Strategy, to allow pupils to reflect on the nature, quality and extent of their learning. It was a new feature of education in England, which primary teachers were not well practised in using and have only gradually become accustomed to preparing for in an effort to help pupils operate it in any way satisfactorily. It is likely to offer similar problems for teachers and pupils in secondary schools, but that should not be a reason for neglecting it.

English teachers will quickly become used to hearing that one of the major transformations expected as a result of the introduction of the English strand of the Key Stage 3 Strategy is the greater attention paid to learning as the starting point for planning and teaching in the subject. If learning is to be regarded so centrally, then pupils – so the argument goes – should be completely familiar with the nature of and reasons for the activities in which they are meant to be engaged. Clearly knowing what they should be doing, and having a better view of the learning embodied in those activities then means that pupils should be given opportunities to question and evaluate the nature of the learning. The plenary session (and it is worth remembering that 'plenary' means 'gathering together', not 'at the end') should be that part of the lesson where pupils share some reflection on what they have done, how well they have done it, and the extent of the learning they have taken from those activities.

In the past, English teachers might have summarised a lesson by asking something like: 'Somebody tell me what we have been doing today, and what we hoped to find out.' Most, however, have not integrated within their work a reflective, evaluative period on a regular basis, with the intention of helping pupils articulate more explicitly what they should be achieving from their studies. It will take practice and gradual revision and evolution over some months before it becomes a natural and comfortable part of most English lessons.

For plenaries to become successful, and properly understood by pupils (but also their teachers), everybody has to be completely clear about the learning being intended in the first place. It is simply not possible to comment on or evaluate the nature of the learning at some point of the lesson, unless all participants are secure about what they should be taking from their studies. Considerable numbers of pupils enjoy and take part enthusiastically in English lessons every day, but a large proportion are never sure about why they might be reading the class text selected for them, or why they were expected to produce the last piece of work they wrote. They need to be more aware of how the reading, writing or speaking tasks planned for them are being expected to contribute to their greater knowledge, control of, and confidence in, linguistic engagements. And it is not good enough for their teachers to tell them what they have been up to; the pupils have to begin expressing for themselves, in a language that they can understand and share, what they have jointly been pursuing to improve their meta-cognitive capabilities.

> The plenary at the end of the session is an opportunity to draw out the learning that has been achieved in the lesson and refer back to the objectives. It also allows a space to celebrate what has been achieved and prepare pupils for the next step.
>
> (DfEE 2001a: 18)

This advice from the *Framework* is worth exploring in greater detail. The assumption that the plenary takes place 'only at the end of the lesson' is mistaken. The plenary can certainly act as a context for summarising what has taken place, and helping to refocus the class's attention on the central themes. But, it can degenerate into little more than a 'show and tell' session, a recount of the events of the lesson, unless teachers and (more accomplished) pupils can steer their thinking back over the lesson in a purposeful way. Other ways in which teachers might use the plenary are:

- while the class is working independently, the teacher might ask everybody to pay attention for a moment, then invite one group to refresh everybody's memory about what they are searching for, and what that group might have discovered;
- the teacher, while working in a 'guided' capacity with one group, sees that they are very successfully pursuing their learning. Everybody is asked to listen to members of the group explaining their approach and successes;

- groups, all pursuing the same learning goals, are invited to devise separate ways of going about their work; representatives from each group are invited to the front of the class to explain the particular methodology employed by that group;
- one or more of the pupils has come across a particular effect or use of language in their own independent reading which relates to the theme or issue being learned. The teacher invites them to relate their findings with the material being studied;
- for a homework, the teacher asks the pupils to consider carefully what they have been doing in class time, and to suggest different approaches or methodologies. A little time is taken from the beginning of the next lesson to consider three or four of these suggestions;
- during independent writing, the class might be stopped for a moment, and all the members of a group asked to read each other's work, before deciding who has most successfully achieved or adhered to the learning objective of the writing.

Lessons playing a full role in assisting pupils to become more evaluative and reflective about their work have to be planned carefully. The plenary is not effective if it is 'dropped' on pupils as a dutiful ending to all lessons. The plenary requires 'shaping' or being prepared for at the start of the lesson, or sequence of lessons. At the beginning of the lesson the teacher could possibly spend a few moments 'framing' the subsequent plenary in the following way: 'I would like you to continue searching for . . . today'; 'Remember that we are looking for . . .'; 'I want you to consider at least two of the writers we have been studying, and be ready to explain how their key ideas are developed through patterns of language'; 'I shall be expecting someone in Jack's group to explain to the rest of us what you have found out about . . . and to suggest why you used that pattern'.

Increasingly, during the past few years, a consensus has grown through educational research that pupils become more effective and motivated learners if they know what it is that they are supposed to be learning. The work of Stoll and Fink (1996), the influential Hay McBer Report to the DfEE (2000) and Udvari-Solner's research (1996) make a strong case for involving pupils in their own learning, by helping them to recognise what they are expected to learn, and how they work as learners.

> The implication is that even in what might be seen as a rather traditional lesson, with little apparent concession being made by the teacher to the individual differences of members of the class, each pupil experiences and defines the meaning of what occurs in their own way. Interpreting the experience in terms of their own mental frames, individuals construct forms of knowledge which may or may not relate to the purposes and understanding of the teacher. Recognising this personal process of meaning-making leads the teacher to have to include in their lesson plans opportunities for self-reflection, in order that pupils can be encouraged to engage with and make personal record of their own developing understandings.
>
> (Udvari-Solner 1996)

The inclusion of some form of plenary, allowing pupils a few moments of stepping aside from their work to cast a critical and evaluative eye over it, is an essential skill that English teachers can do much to promote.

In the final analysis, of course, a four part lesson structure will not in itself improve or in any way change what transpires in English lessons. All teachers could slavishly adopt the recommended version, and continue to do what they have always done. Improving the pace of lessons, concentrating on the learning outcomes, varying the experiences pupils encounter, bringing about different ways of making meaning, determining to improve the reading, writing, and speaking and listening capabilities of their pupils, are all improvements depending on teachers' attitudes. The success of the four part lesson requires the same sort of commitment, ultimately, to allow it to make a real difference to what went before.

4 Rethinking Reading using the *Framework* at Key Stage 3

If the work currently transforming English, literacy and language skills in Key Stages 1 and 2 is to be given real status and importance, it has to be recognised and built on by teaching colleagues in Key Stage 3. However well individual teachers have prepared their pupils during Year 6, recipient English teachers undertaking lessons with Year 7 pupils should assume that the young people sitting in front of them have, at the very least, been familiarised with the Year 6 programme in the Literacy Strategy *Framework for Teaching* (DfEE 1998). From that one development alone, English teaching will have moved on a significant stage.

As was discussed in earlier chapters, English teaching has traditionally been hampered (some might claim 'enhanced') by a number of practices which have steadily evolved, over time, without any firm centre. Roger Knight, an English academic at Leicester University, and editor of The English Association's magazine *The Use of English* has no doubt:

> For me, in recent years, thinking about and teaching 'English' has often had to be against the grain of official prescription and public pronouncement. This is not a matter of choice but conviction. The heart of this conviction is that 'English' cannot *be* 'English' unless it is rooted in and unified by the study of literature. Therein lies its claim to be a distinctive curriculum subject.
>
> (Knight 1996)

This unequivocal statement would seem to be a summation of the sorts of 'objectives' suggested by Fred Inglis in 1969. The first five were:

> The teaching of English may be seen by the teacher (and for preference the pupil), as a matter of cherishing and guiding his [sic] pupils in strenuous efforts:
>
> 1. To train the capacity to evaluate and adjust an individual scheme of values in relation to personal literary experience.
> 2. To cultivate the imaginative power not to 'think about' but to 'realise' and 'become' a complex experience given in words, e.g. a poem.
> 3. To encourage a vivid personal delight in reading literature as a serious and recreative present.
> 4. To train a pupil in a disciplined and sensitive attention to language in all forms, so that imprecision and inflation is known for what it is.
> 5. To teach the ability to describe and evaluate individual experience (including literary) in words, precisely and with audacity, cunning, passion and resourcefulness.
>
> (Inglis 1969)

The Bullock Report (DES 1975) attempted to pull the various strands of thinking about English together into some sort of organised coherence, but merely recognised the different 'factions' shaping the way the subject was approached in a range of different institutions:

> Some teachers see English as an instrument of personal growth, going so far as to declare that 'English is about growing up'. They believe that the activities which it involves give it a special opportunity to develop the pupil's sensibility and help him to adjust to the various pressures of life. Others feel that the emphasis should be placed on direct instruction in the skills of reading and writing and that a concern for the pupil's personal development should not obscure this priority. There are those who would prefer English to be an instrument of social change. For them the ideal of 'bridging the social gap' by sharing a common culture is unacceptable, not simply as having failed to work but as implying the superiority of 'middle class culture'. Of course, even where a teacher subscribes to a particular approach he does not necessarily pursue it exclusively, neglecting all else.
>
> (DES 1975: para. 1.4)

Brian Cox, chairing a committee preparing the grounds and content for the first officially published curriculum in English studies, also acknowledged these, and other, preoccupations in 1989. He made mention of five views of English teaching: personal growth, cross-curricular, adult needs, cultural heritage and cultural analysis. Yet, as Chris Davies (1996) points out:

> These categories have been useful in demonstrating the increasingly plural nature of attitudes to English teaching, but the quality of analysis is shaky: 'cultural heritage', 'personal growth' and 'adult needs' are simply different aspects of one view of English, all of which implicitly or explicitly take for granted the privileged status of English literature, but in ways that vary according to a long-established perception of the differing needs of students from different social classes. To a large extent, therefore, these do not really represent different views at all, whereas a 'cultural analysis' viewpoint is so firmly opposed to beliefs about the inherent superiority of particular forms of language and literature that it could never be reconciled with the previous three. In addition it is meaningless to talk of a 'cross-curricular' view of the English subject area, or of any particular subject. The whole point – which the Bullock Report understood quite clearly in trying to establish a cross-curricular view of learning to use the English language – is that the relationship between the English subject area and the rest of literacy learning needed to be examined and developed.
>
> (Davies 1996)

The 1990s became a period when, with government mismanagement and ignorance stamping all over their efforts and beliefs, English teachers hung on with relief to the few positive gains they perceived the Cox Committee had offered them when they had been expecting the worst. As it became clear that successive Conservative administrations, feeling badly betrayed by Cox, set up all manner of 'review' apparatus to erode the original structures and content of the 1990 National Curriculum Orders, English teachers had no room or time for exploring and reflecting on the developments taking place in other countries around the world to do with the study of, and better understanding of, language.

There was certainly no consensus about the relationship of literature and language in English studies (although one remarkable trend was the fast-growing popularity of the A level language paper), and while reading, writing, speaking and listening had been given separate, although fuzzy, identities in the English curriculum, there was no understood central notion about what pupils were expected ultimately to learn and take away from their English lessons. Anybody doubting this statement should consider carefully the current contents of the English and English literature GCSE syllabuses.

The sorts of trends in secondary English lessons, observed by Bullock:

> But we refer here in particular to the notion of English in the secondary school as almost exclusively a source of material for personal response to social issues. Literature is experienced largely in the form of extracts and is filleted for its social yield. Talk is shepherded into the area of publicised questions of acute issues of the day. The writing that emerges from both is to a large extent judged for its success by the measure of commitment it seems to reveal. Genuine personal response in such circumstances is not easy to express.
>
> (DES 1975)

and Davies:

> It is not easy to identify a single overriding learning aim for a particular English lesson; pupils study poems in order to develop their oral skills or their awareness of the process of language change; pupils write science fiction in order to develop their descriptive skills, or their ability to handle the conventions of dialogue . . .
>
> Whatever the learning aim, English teaching predominantly involves the study or production of texts of an imaginative/creative/expressive kind
>
> (Davies 1996)

do not show any movement towards addressing the fundamental questions raised by Professor Henry Widdowson, a member of the Kingman Committee inquiring into the teaching of English language, in his minority 'Note of Reservation' in the Report published in 1988:

- How will literacy be used in people's lives in the twenty-first century?
- What is English in the school curriculum for?
- What is the nature of the relationship between English as a curriculum subject and literacy?

The question has largely been ducked; and preoccupation with the techniques and management of raising standards has served to obscure it even more. Discussion of literacy and its relationship to English in the school curriculum, appears to have been concerned very little with identifying what young people need to be able to do, or to know, in order to participate fully in increasingly complex and globalized social and economic worlds.

> (Poulson 1998)

All this background has been a necessary preparation for suggesting very strongly that it lies within the power of individual English departments, in discussion with the teachers of other subjects, to begin answering the questions set out above. A literacy programme can only be worth while where it is genuinely designed to contribute to the pupils' needs, in an immediate and long-term view. The school can frame its literacy experiences very clearly to serve the learning purposes and ends it espouses. Those learning purposes have to meet more than just the assessment mechanisms the school chooses or is obliged to conduct. Therefore, the school should not only be implementing a 'literacy strategy' because the Government has made it a priority, but because the school really ought to be developing and sharing an idea about the ways that language is making all learning possible. The English department has to be a key player in all those discussions and decisions. So, even if the Government, in the guise of the National Literacy managers, has failed yet again to face up to answering the vitally important questions of what English is 'for', and what relationship it shares with an idea called 'literacy', single teams of English teachers should begin to address these concerns in their own ways. Because the objectives expected to be covered by all pupils have been published, as an entitlement, in the *Framework*, the disputes about these questions should not be as far flung and widespread as they have been in the past. The *Framework for Teaching English: Years 7, 8 and 9* also offers support to these suggestions:

> English teachers have a leading role in providing pupils with the knowledge, skills and understanding they need to read, write, speak and listen effectively, but this document also addresses other subject staff. Language is the prime medium through which pupils learn and express themselves across the curriculum, and all teachers have a stake in effective literacy.
>
> (DfEE 2001a: 10)

In a review of two books about the history of English, Geoff Barton, an English teacher who has regularly used and explored the opportunities offered by the secondary English strand in the Key Stage 3 Strategy, and written enthusiastically of their potential, writes:

> One important quibble, however, about both books. They focus on teaching, which, at the end of the twentieth century, isn't the real issue. The issue is learning. And the correlation between teaching and learning isn't always as inevitable as we might hope. Learning needs to be at the heart of the English agenda because teaching follows from it. Without a clear framework for the way children acquire and then develop language, for the way reading and writing skills develop, teachers can get locked into approaches that are ineffective.
>
> (Barton 1999)

I will go further: a school can invest any amount of time and interest developing approaches to literacy and English, but unless the teachers have a clear idea about how pupils learn language, employ language in their learning, and make progress with learning language, then literacy skills will not improve.

Intrinsic to knowing how pupils make progress with learning language has to be a notion, known and understood by all the teachers in a school, of what a 'reader', or 'writer' or 'speaker' or 'listener' might be in the first place. If the school is to improve 'reading', or 'writing' or 'speaking' or 'listening' – and all teachers in the school (see paragraph 10 of the *Framework* quoted above) should be players in that programme –

then knowing what it is that needs to be improved would seem a reasonable starting point. Would subject teachers involved in other areas set out to 'improve' their pupils as chemists, or technologists or musicians without having already established which areas of chemistry, technology or music those pupils would need to learn? Just because literacy (the ability to read, write, speak and listen to make clear meanings in a range of contexts) is part of being a better chemist, technologist or musician, is absolutely no reason why the same principles should not apply. The uncertain relationship between English and literacy discussed at the beginning of this chapter could possibly be more purposefully addressed and made more secure through these shared considerations.

What is a reader?

In 2000 I published a book *Teaching Reading in Secondary Schools* because it was my perception that not much teaching of reading was actually provided for pupils beyond the age of 11. Any attention given to reading in the secondary school mostly came about as a result of some pupils being diagnosed with undeveloped reading skills, usually leading to the provision of a 'catch up' programme of a limited kind. My book was aimed primarily at English teachers:

> Reading is not taught in most secondary schools in England. Considerable numbers of activities in connection with books and other sorts of texts take place in classrooms, but these are not usually directed towards the improvement and growth of pupils' reading, except in a very limited sense.

> (Dean 2000)

If English teachers were not teaching reading before the introduction of the Key Stage 3 Strategy, then teachers of other subjects were certainly not conducting lessons in reading either. Yet all, or certainly the vast majority of, teachers expect pupils to read textual material of some kind in most of their lessons. It would then be reasonable to encourage all teachers to have some idea of what it means to be a 'reader', and how that 'readerliness' can be improved within the context of the demands of each curriculum subject. Not every teacher, however knowledgeable or experienced they might be, can read and make immediate meaning from every text in their own language. There are always examples we will never have previously come across, or that have only specialised currency and circulation.

English teachers might try making sense of the following passage without too much practice and constant rereading:

> The fat body of the fifth stage larva of *Calpodes ethlius* undergoes sequential organelle specific autophagy as a first step in the cell remodelling necessary for metamorphosis to the pupa (Locke and Collins, 1965, Locke and McMahon 1971). This autophagy begins at about 36 hr before pupation and coincides with the time after which an abdomen isolated from the thorax by ligation will still pupate. After this critical period (Locke 1970) the abdominal tissues continue to develop in the absence of further ecdysone from the prothoracic glands. The coincidence between the critical period for the operation of the prothoracic glands and the start of autophagy, and the

fact that fat body autophagy occurs in isolated pre-critical period abdomens when injected with ecdysone (Collins 1969), suggested that autophagy is induced by ecdysone.

(Dean 1978)

If that is a bit too difficult, try this piece:

Seattle jumped in front with runs off Pettyjohn in the second and third innings. Ed Sprague led off the second with a single, took second when Pettyjohn hit David Bell, then scored on Stan Javier's single to right. It appeared that Juan Encarnacion's throw had a chance to get Sprague at the plate, but it was cut off by first baseman Shane Halter. Brett Boone led off the third inning with a double, moved up on John Olerud's grounder and scored on Mike Cameron's lineout to left.

(*USA Today* 3 August 2001)

Some of the words are familiar; we can say everything out loud by decoding, or even say them to ourselves silently, but the meaning is likely to take a long time to emerge, after a little worrying of the text, if at all. The reader has to establish all sorts of background information, and 'frame' the information if engagement is to be made and substantial, not just partial, meaning taken from the passage. It would help enormously if the reader realised that the first passage concerned advanced biological research about what causes changes in one species of insect to bring about pupation, while the second is a baseball report in an American newspaper.

The above examples are included to stimulate some reflection by all teachers about the nature of reading. Over a period of about ten years I worked with teachers of different subjects, exploring what I regarded as essential 'reading knowledges': those skills or abilities required by all successful readers to enable the most effective understanding and extraction of meaning of many sorts of text. These skills have to:

- apply to all readers, regardless of age or general, overall ability;
- apply to reading in different subjects, or areas of interest, not just relating to the reading of fiction/literature;
- be possible for teachers in different phases of education to share, and to introduce to their pupils;
- cover a range of possible textual interactions leading to better meaning making and genuine response;
- be capable of improvement;
- be understandable to all readers.

The suggested list of these abilities, or 'qualities', was published in *Teaching Reading in Secondary Schools* (Dean 2000), but is reproduced in slightly amended form below:

This school or subject department believes that:

1. a reader knows that reading is a complex, intellectual endeavour, requiring the reader to draw on a range of active meaning-making skills;
2. a reader searches previous knowledge of other texts to enable the effective meaning-making of the text being read;
3. a reader is aware that texts are constructed for particular purposes, for identifiable audiences and within recognisable text types, or genres;

4. a reader can usually predict the ways texts are likely to work and develop, and can use reading to confirm or adjust those predictions, depending on how typically the text unfolds;

5. a reader is critically active before becoming involved in the substantial body of any text;

6. a reader is able to activate a growing repertoire of critical and analytical questions in engagements with new and unfamiliar texts;

7. a reader increasingly knows how to interact appropriately with a variety of text types/genres for particular purposes;

8. a reader is aware that an important way of demonstrating reading progression is through raising more complex questions about the same text;

9. a reader is aware that learning to read is a life-long process;

10. a reader is aware that other readers do not always read and make meanings in the same ways;

11. a reader can explain why a text might not satisfy the task to which it has been put, or been rejected unfinished;

12. a reader knows that reading improves through monitoring and reflection on own ability and progress.

These may not, by any means, be the only considerations that academics concerned with the development and teaching of reading would want to consider (they do not, for instance, mention directly anything about pleasure and enjoyment). They may not be the most helpful set of criteria any group of teachers might devise, from a cold start, by themselves. They are, however, a practical useful starting point for teachers involved in teaching the whole range of subjects on offer in any school, to set off a common discussion about how they could all contribute to their pupils' reading progress. If English and literacy are to have a meaningful and significant relationship, capable of raising standards of literacy and language awareness across the whole school, then an overlap of shared concerns, of the sort provided by the list above, is essential.

One important word of warning: the following pages necessarily focus on only one aspect of reading – the decoding and meaning-making processes applied to published texts (usually black marks in the form of words, on white paper). 'Reading' could be, and is in many different circumstances, interpreted in a much broader manner, including the interpretation of, for instance, visual texts, such as television and video. Definitions of 'literacy' in individual schools would not be complete without some attention being paid to those sorts of textual materials through which pupils gain inevitable knowledge of their world.

The implications of each of these 'qualities' or 'statements' of the reader are worth exploring in more detail.

1. a reader knows that reading is a complex, intellectual endeavour, requiring the reader to draw on a range of active meaning-making skills;

Readers 'know' that they have to bring a number of probing and critical skills to the engagement with any text. Quite simply, they have to 'put their brains in gear'! Poor readers often poke about at a piece of text, hoping that some meaning will emerge. Developing and good readers are aware that they have to begin:

- making relationships with previously encountered texts;
- looking for clues;
- seeking patterns;
- considering the context (e.g. 'is this a story?', 'is this information I require?', 'does this relate to the subject matter in which I am engaged?', etc.).

Is there a characteristic of the writing possible to pin down and use for further understanding? Whatever the problems of the piece, the reader should be able to set out ways of approaching and solving them, to get the reading process fully underway.

> When reading with a class it could be helpful to run through some tactics for tackling textual material for less experienced readers, or a competent class might be asked to describe the approaches they are employing.

2. a reader searches previous knowledge of other texts to enable the effective meaning-making of the text being read;

All reading is 'intertextual'. The meanings we make in all that we read are dependent on what we have read before. At the very least, a reader has to establish whether the text under consideration is familiar, or whether it is material presented in a wholly new way. The subject or content of the text might be different, but the patterns of language, presentation and text development could well resemble those of familiar examples. Somehow or another, when reading, we are reaching back to previous textual experiences, building on and adding to what we have found out before. And the textual experiences do not have to be published in books; they could be in the form of a film, a television programme, an oral story heard at some time in the past, etc.

> When reading with pupils it can be helpful to discover from them where they have seen texts like the one being studied in other circumstances. Can they relate the current text to previous reading experiences in any way?

3. a reader is aware that texts are constructed for particular purposes, for identifiable audiences and within recognisable text types, or genres;

Writers create texts to fulfil certain purposes. They are usually written to, for instance, instruct, report, inform, discuss, persuade, recount, etc. A single text might recount, report, argue and provoke at the same time, but the reader will only take the fullest meanings from the text if alive and alert to all those intentions as the text is appraised. Some texts are narrating stories intended to amuse (comedy), or tease (thrillers), or comment on scientific advances (science fiction). Meaning begins to become clearer as the reader uncovers what it was the writer was attempting to do. Pupils should, of course, be increasingly introduced to a wide range of different text types or genres, to accumulate an increasing repertoire of questions to put to these texts.

Teachers reading a text with a class should spend a few moments checking with those pupils if they can establish what the text was constructed to do. In that rudimentary way they can then make such a question a natural part of the reader's approach to all texts.

4. a reader can usually predict the ways texts are likely to work and develop, and can use reading to confirm or adjust those predictions, depending on how typically the text unfolds;

A fiction text will usually differ from a non-fiction text in a large number of ways; in terms of presentation; layout; vocabulary; purpose. Reading fiction usually means that pupils start at the beginning, and follow clues and cues to construct stages of development. Non-fiction texts will have organisational features in keeping with their purposes, but most types will not require that sort of developing, cumulative, stage by stage approach. To find the best ways around the text might require helpful signposts, such as an index, or contents table and subheadings. The information required might be discretely gathered in one identifiable space, but parts of the information might be spread about the text, requiring gathering and sorting on the part of the reader.

Depending on whether the class is involved with a fiction or non-fiction text, teachers could check with pupils how a fiction might be developing, and the evidence to suggest how it might continue; or pupils might be asked what they expect of a particular way that non-fiction has been presented.

5. a reader is critically active before becoming involved in the substantial body of any text;

Even the youngest readers begin quickly to realise that certain sorts of published text have their own characteristics. Fiction books mostly have drawn pictures on the cover, picking out an incident, sometimes of a dramatic kind, from the narrative. Non-fiction usually has a photograph or a 'real-life' drawing, depicting realistic scenes from life. As readers grow in knowledge and sophistication, they begin to recognise that certain sorts of title are likely to suggest associated text types, for example 'How to' books mostly contain explanations. Adults seek out authors or covers of recognisable particular kinds on the shelves of libraries and bookshops, aware that the contents of such books will align with their already developed tastes and reading preferences. Readers can save considerable time by not engaging with texts that are unlikely to meet their demands, so the more they can tell about the text from first acquaintance, the better.

Pupils can be assisted in developing this skill in their classroom by teachers spending a moment considering the cover, the context in which the text is expected to be read, and checking against pupils' responses and predictions.

6. a reader is able to activate a growing repertoire of critical and analytical questions in engagements with new and unfamiliar texts;

Many young people, when confronted with texts for the first time, have not developed systematic approaches necessary to gain reasonably rapid access to their contents and purposes. Faced with difficulties of that sort, they feel ignorant or excluded, and turn their attention away from the text, sometimes claiming that it is 'boring'. Pupils have to begin gaining the confidence and wherewithal to engage with increasingly difficult texts, but such strategies have to be based on processes and skills they can control and call on as required.

In the Reading module of the English department training file (DfEE 2001f), published by the National Literacy central team, is an appendix listing a number of suggested typical word, sentence and text level questions pupils should become more familiar asking as part of any reading engagement. These questions are not just suitable to put to fiction or literary texts, but all sorts of examples. Teachers familiarising themselves with these questions and applying them regularly to their reading activities will be making a major contribution to pupils' reading competence.

> Teachers should select, on a regular basis, a question or two to put, with their pupils, to different examples of text, to enable their classes to apply these same questions for themselves.

7. a reader increasingly knows how to interact appropriately with a variety of text types/genres for particular purposes;

At its simplest, this means that pupils reading a non-chronological, non-fiction report text do not attempt to read it in the same manner as fiction. As pupils develop more critical skills, and can handle more issues in text, so they also know more confidently how to respond to, and even work with the text in order to gain the most appropriate benefits from it. Pupils working with poetry, for instance, need to learn techniques to enable them to discover meanings in many ways.

Pupils have to realise that meanings are not immediately available even for experienced and capable readers. Some texts have to be reread, or require different questions to be asked of them. Discourses are structured in a vast number of ways, and pupils have to be able to practise working within as broad a range of structures as possible.

> A team of teachers comprising a school staff should analyse the types of reading their pupils are likely to encounter in Key Stage 3, and spend some time identifying which subjects might be giving particular attention to which sorts of texts, to ensure the broadest possible coverage and practice.

8. a reader is aware that an important way of demonstrating reading progression is through raising more complex questions about the same text;

Texts are not necessarily intrinsically easy, or difficult. Certainly some are more densely structured and contain a more specialist vocabulary than others. Yet, children often surprise us by seeming to find no problems dealing fluently with texts deemed 'tough', if they have been driven by enthusiasm for the topic or some other motivation. Even Billy Casper stole a book about hawks from his local library!

Some departments might operate a 'readability' survey, but they are not always reliable, and they could prevent some readers being allowed access to necessary texts. Pupils have to be aware that their own commitment to the text is one starting point for eventual reading success; they also need a background of possible questions or lines of enquiry to take. The only way that certain pupils will ever make real progress is by being guided through the methods which actually lead to that development. Some pupils will be naturally more adept at reading certain sorts of texts; they will also need to reflect on and attempt to analyse why some other text types present difficulties. The problems are not always to do with the print on the page.

> If the school is establishing a policy for reading, it is likely that it will also want to think about what constitutes 'progression' in reading. Teachers in the classroom can help their pupils become more confident and better prepared readers by encouraging them to become more reflective about the difficulties presented by certain sorts of texts – and how pupils can successfully address them.

9. a reader is aware that learning to read is a life-long process;

A few readers of this book could probably make immediate sense of the two extracts exemplified on page 65. Most adult readers, however, will be unfamiliar with such styles and content, and a single contact with the texts would be insufficient time to draw much meaning from them. Even then, the reader might find it hard to emulate the texts by attempting to write in that manner; much more practice and acquaintanceship would be essential. Even texts that readers have become comfortable with sometimes surprise. We sometimes think we have discovered all there is to be known about a familiar text, only for somebody to then point out a meaning we have never thought of before!

> Teachers could offer some reading experiences in the classroom to ensure that the pupils have been given time to discover and discuss the issues raised by a text unfamiliar to most pupils in the class. This would be a deliberate and worthwhile way of practising the objectives designed to encourage 'Reading for meaning' (Year 7 Text Level objectives 6, 7 and 8/Year 8 objective 4), as well as a necessary developing skill in its own right.

10. a reader is aware that other readers do not always read and make meanings in the same ways;

Each one of us has a unique literacy biography. Everyone experiences and has experienced texts in quite different ways, and we bring unique personal life events to texts, which fashion and change the meanings we subsequently take from them. By way of example, offer the word 'dog' to a group of pupils. Each one will vaguely have an idea of a quadruped, with a head and tail, but from that point on all perceptions will differ. The actual dog could be tall or short; black, brown or white; playful or threatening; hairy or smooth; like a puppy or elderly; or all the shades of difference between those extremes.

In school subjects pupils regularly come across words that are spelt and pronounced in the same way, but have different meanings in specific contexts; for example, the word 'field' means quite different things to a geographer, a physics teacher and a PE teacher. Katherine Perera, the linguist, writes:

> An additional problem with such familiar words is that the writer may take them for granted and not explain or highlight them in the text. In *The Developing World: Geography Two*, the following seemingly familiar words occur in one nine page unit of work: estate, roots, grub, nap, battery, stock, cake, mean, litter, relief.
>
> It seems likely that a twelve year old pupil will be able to assign a meaning to each of these words, but it may not be the technical sense that the writer intends. For although these words are not capitalized in the text (unlike the obviously specialist vocabulary), they all have technical rather than everyday meanings, i.e. estate: farmland/roots: root-crops (potatoes)/grub: to uproot a hedge/nap: pile on cloth/battery: shed for hens/stock: cattle/cake: cattle-food etc.
>
> (Perera 1984)

The assumption by some teachers is that the particular meaning in their own context is the one the pupils know!

Pupils, like all other readers, also associate different events with texts. Very young children who have recently experienced a relative dying will react much more sensitively to a book about loss and mourning, such as John Burningham's 'Granpa'. Children who have been taken to visit a castle, cathedral, or other site likely to crop up in a story, or historical setting, will have a far more vivid sense of the part such a setting can play.

> It is essential, in all reading situations in all lessons, that some time is set aside to allow pupils to check through any key vocabulary. Teachers should establish that pupils have a common set of meanings for those words. Pupils might sometimes like to suggest what feelings, memories or associations a text brings to mind for them.

11. a reader can explain why a text might not satisfy the task to which it has been put, or been rejected unfinished;

Pupils will sometimes choose a text, perhaps because it is stored in the appropriate section of the library, but discover that it is not able to satisfy the task they are pursuing. They might, alternatively, have been asked to read a work of fiction, but come to the conclusion after a few chapters that they really do not want to continue reading it. Schools should include, as part of their teaching reading programme, methods of assisting pupils in articulating the decisions they have made about texts. This issue is really concerned with improving pupils' sense of choice. Much of what pupils read in school has been decided for them; they make relatively little selection of the materials they are expected to study. Yet, becoming an independent reader means being able to make good selections of whole texts, or parts of texts, for particular purposes. Large numbers of English departments decide which works of fiction pupils will encounter in the classroom, so introducing a larger element of choice will change some of the normal practices (and resource implications) of 'reading lessons'.

Pupils need regular reminders about why they have been asked to engage with particular texts, and for what reasons. Even when a text has been assigned by a teacher, it does not mean that the pupil should give up thinking critically about it, and deciding if it is the most effective resource for the task.

12. a reader knows that reading improves through monitoring and reflection on own ability and progress.

All pupils should be assessed on their reading progression, but that assessment can only be helpful if it is based on reading in a range of contexts. In the section on plenary sessions in Chapter 3, there is also an argument about why pupils should be expected to develop self-monitoring strategies, which should also recognise the different sorts of reading skills being deployed in different learning contexts. Self-monitoring techniques should be increasingly used for most learning enterprises in Key Stage 3, and if teachers are more aware of the many issues related to reading development they should be able to promote these sorts of skills in the whole gamut of lessons.

A school giving full attention to the overview of reading 'qualities' outlined in this section will be in a much better position to publish and share a reading policy likely to influence all teachers in all subjects. Some of the 'statements' or 'qualities' readily translate into policy terms, but others need only minimal modification to be shaped into a strategic approach. From this set of statements, a policy could be created which sets out the school's aims to enable pupils to:

- realise how important reading is to literacy progression and the capacity to learn;
- read fluently and with understanding across the broadest possible range of texts;
- use all the available clues in texts to search for meaning;
- recognise that the makers of texts devise them for a variety of clear purposes, and for known audiences;
- develop a range of reading strategies to make the fullest possible meaning in individual texts and across a range of texts;
- read for different purposes (e.g. for pleasure, to find information, to establish models for own writing, to explore the views and attitudes of others, etc.);
- make increasingly realistic and accurate predictions about texts;
- make progress as readers in a number of ways, for the rest of their lives;
- become increasingly reflective about their own reading development.

The literacy and English strands of the Key Stage 3 Strategy will not supply a school with these underpinning fundamental foundations for improving literacy across the whole curriculum. Schools have to devise their own guiding principles and practise what they advocate if they are to develop approaches to literacy that are likely to last.

Reading in English

The English strand of the Key Stage 3 Strategy offers all English departments the opportunity to review their current reading practices, and a chance to attempt new ways of planning and teaching reading. As in all areas of the Strategy the focus should be on *learning*. Texts should not be included in class activities as ends in themselves. They should, as often as possible, be the vehicles to bring about improved learning in some area of reading. Merely enabling young people to acquire a long list of titles that have been read is not the best use of classroom time.

English teachers have traditionally wanted their pupils to enjoy reading, and pursue that pleasure by reading on, or finding other texts for themselves in their own time. In most English classrooms a 'reading together' text has often been chosen for the pupils because the teacher has enjoyed it. This can be a very 'hit and miss' business, with a very limiting effect on introducing pupils to a wide range of texts from which they begin developing the skills to choose for themselves. The English strand of the Strategy offers an opportunity for teachers to rethink this method of reading provision and resourcing.

English teachers could be asking themselves:

- What sorts of readers does this department want to encourage?
- What is 'reading'?
- What does the 'teaching' of reading mean in this department?
- What are the different sorts of reading the whole school should be teaching?
- Which areas of 'reading' can we realistically teach properly within the remit of our work?
- How will we know that our 'readers' have made progress?
- What contribution to 'reading' do the other subject departments make?
- Which resources will be most supportive in the learning of reading?
- What would be the best classroom and grouping arrangements to support the learning of reading?

There are different sorts of reading for pupils to learn, and they are the responsibility of the whole school. English departments have traditionally been concerned with the reading of literature, and the *Framework for Teaching English* (DfEE 2001a) recognises that tradition, but also points out the alternatives on page 11, where a table sets out the broad overview of reading objectives:

- Research and study skills
- Reading for meaning
- Understanding the author's craft
- Study of literary texts

These are, however, a very vague and wide-ranging set of statements requiring closer detail before a department can begin planning for real learning.

One of the best starting points for considering the questions suggested above could be for English teachers to look carefully at the objectives for teaching reading in the *Framework* in Years 7, 8 and 9. Thinking about these, and also taking notice of the requirements of the Key Stage 3 National Curriculum English Orders, would offer substantial ground for rethinking.

Research and study skills

There are 12 objectives listed in total relating to research and study skills across the three year programme. They are an identifiable, related group, building in difficulty, possible to share and discuss with all teachers in the school. English teachers could spend a little time supporting and even setting off learning in these objectives, but their continuation and development really ought to belong to all colleagues:

Year 7 Text level – Reading
2. use appropriate reading strategies to extract particular information, e.g. *highlighting, scanning;*
3. compare and contrast the ways information is presented in different forms, e.g. *web page, diagrams, prose;*
4. make brief, clearly organised notes of key points for later use;

(DfEE 2001a: 24)

The likelihood is that these skills will be used very regularly in all subjects, and if there was an insistence on their use across the curriculum, with attention paid to their supported improvement, all staff would be genuinely supporting each other.

Reading for meaning

The objectives offered in this and the following section, across all three years of the Strategy, have the potential to lead to real changes in the ways reading is taught, and learned, in English. The first objective is very powerful:

6. adopt active reading approaches to engage with and make sense of texts e.g. *visualising, predicting, empathising and relating to own experience;*

(DfEE 2001a: 24)

'Active' is a word demanding close attention and consideration in the context of reading. Too many reading experiences in classrooms fail to engage pupils, and boys particularly often do not know how to make a relationship with texts they are supposed to be studying, leading to their diminishing commitment to them. If the 'active reading' objective is combined with a number of the following examples, an English teacher can establish powerful ways in the classroom, and beyond, of aiding pupils to extract enormous meaning from the texts being studied:

Year 7 Reading
Reading for meaning
7. identify the main points, processes or ideas in a text and how they are sequenced and developed by the writer;
8. infer and deduce meanings using evidence in the text, identifying where and how meanings are implied;

Understanding the author's craft

12. comment, using appropriate terminology on how writers convey setting, character and mood through word choice and sentence structure . . .
14. recognise how writers' language choices can enhance meaning e.g. *repetition,*

emotive vocabulary, varied sentence structure or line length, sound effects;

15. trace the ways in which a writer structures a text to prepare a reader for the ending, and comment on the effectiveness of the ending;

(DfEE 2001a: 24)

Active reading might take a number of forms, and one or two are considered in the following sections. In *Teaching Reading in Secondary Schools* (Dean 2000), I suggest a method of very active bonding with the text, possible by all readers, based on these objectives. An illustration of this is given below.

Exemplar Study of *Holes* by Louis Sacher (1998)

This wonderful book, recently imported from the USA, is already well known to many teenage English readers; one of those special books recommended by young people to their friends. It is a story of injustice, suffering, friendship, mystery, optimism, courage and coincidence, with remarkable twists, told in an amusing manner, in a witty and intelligent style. It is the sort of text described by Italo Calvino, the Italian writer, as a 'fat book', even though it is only a little over 200 pages long! It is a book about books and reading; a good choice for helping readers to reflect on the reading process while still enjoying the experience.

The most supportive study of texts, particularly for less confident readers, can often develop from comparative considerations. I have two editions of the text in front of me: one, in paperback, published by Bloomsbury in 2000; the second, published by Collins Cascades, in hardback (for classroom use, which again is worth exploring with your pupils) with no date (but probably 2001). Remarkably, they have very similar covers. Books reprinted by other publishers mostly have new covers drawn for them, in a marketing, updating exercise. This would not be appropriate in the case of *Holes*, as your pupils will quickly discover and explain. Both covers feature prominently a fierce looking lizard-like creature, with green patches and long claws. This lizard is juxtaposed against a halved cover design; one half a brown tinted photograph of scrub wasteland, and the other a bright blue, almost cloudless sky. These cover designs are well worth exploring closely and encouraging discussion about. As well as both covers naming the novel and the author (both sets of proper names in small case letters on the Bloomsbury edition), the Bloomsbury text has the words, '"Unmistakably powerful" Philip Pullman, *The Guardian*'. What do the words mean? Why are they there? Who is Philip Pullman and why should his comments have relevance? Why *The Guardian*?

Step 1

At this stage (try to ensure that pupils keep their whole attention on just the front covers) pupils could talk together, sharing every detail of what they can see, and why the publisher might have included what can be observed, and what it might mean. Encourage the pupils to:

- suggest what the book might be about;
- suggest, however wildly it might seem at the moment, what the plot might be;

- raise an agreed number (3/5/10 depending on their reading maturity/confidence) of questions they want to have answered as they read on.

Keep a record of the predictions and the questions being raised about the text in personalised envelopes, to which the pupils have access as the text is read.

The next stage is to look carefully at the back covers. Both again make reference to the lizard creature, although slightly differently. The Bloomsbury edition is more densely printed, with the whole of the back cover saturated in white text on the wasteland/sky background. The legend is:

> Stanley Yelnats' family has a history of bad luck, so he isn't too surprised when a miscarriage of justice sends him to a boys' juvenile detention centre. At Camp Green Lake the boys must dig a hole a day, five feet deep, five feet across, in the dried up lake bed. The Warden claims the labour is character building, but it is a lie. Stanley must dig up the truth.

The Collins edition offers a much shorter outline:

> Stanley Yelnats' sentence is to dig hole after hole in the burning desert at a juvenile detention centre like no other. As his story unfolds, so does that of his ancestors. Will the family curse work itself out before it kills Stanley?

Step 2

At this stage make a comparison between the two summaries. Suggest ways in which they differ, and how they make the reader think about the central concerns of the two versions of the same book. Look closely at Stanley's name (somebody in the class will make the connection!). Why might the book be called *Holes*? Are there other meanings of 'Holes' apparent at this point? Encourage the pupils to:

- readjust their plot suggestions, and offer a new version;
- suggest how the book might end;
- check whether any of their previous questions have now already been answered;
- raise 3 to 5 new questions to be answered through further reading.

There is more printed text on both back covers. The Bloomsbury edition, published some months before the Collins, has extracts from three reviews:

> Written with a crystalline prose and simplicity of style it is startlingly original. There is not one false sentence.
>
> (*The Independent on Sunday*)

> This is a story of friendship with the cleverest of plot twists, and descriptions so vivid you can feel the heat of Stanley's desert prison burning off the page. A total must-read.
>
> (*The Times*)

> An exceptionally funny and generous book that is also a tightly plotted detective novel.
>
> (*The Guardian*)

The Collins version repeats the title at the top of the back cover, then announces:

'Winner of the Newbery Medal'. (Can pupils look up Newbery Medal on the Internet?) That is followed by:

> An essential read for young people . . . personally I cannot wait to try it out in the classroom.
>
> (Bruce Butt, *English and Media* magazine)

> This is the story of friendship with the cleverest of plot twists, and descriptions so vivid you can feel the heat of Stanley's desert prison burning off the page. A total must-read.
>
> *(The Times)*

Step 3

At this stage your class might consider why these pieces of prose have been chosen to be reproduced on the back of the books. What differences can be discerned between them, even though they both include the same quotation? Who has made these statements, and in which circumstances? Can we possibly tell anything about the intended reading contexts of each of the texts?

Reading of the substantial body of the text can now begin! However, teachers will remind their pupils, who may not have worked before in this manner, that they have, in fact, been reading very carefully up to this point. Before getting under way, it is always worth making a quick exploration of a fiction text, to establish how it has been structured or divided. Such knowledge can alert the reader very early to ways of ascertaining meaning; 'Day 1' or 'January', for instance, suggests that what will follow is likely to be in diary or journal form. This particular book seems to have two 'parts': 'Part One – You are entering Camp Green Lake', and, following Chapter 28, 'Part Two – The Last Hole'. The class might be asked the significance of 'You are entering Camp Green Lake'; where they might see those words; what sorts of effect they could have on characters in the story, etc.

Step 4

At this point the pupils could be invited to undertake a really active piece of reading, through a procedure I called 'close language study' in *Teaching Reading in Secondary Schools* (Dean 2000). George Keith, who first modelled this procedure in his chapter 'Noticing Grammar' in the QCA (1999) publication *Not Whether But How: Teaching Grammar in English at Key Stages 3 and 4*, writes:

> Notice that the context for looking at grammar is the weaving of a narrative text – how it is done and what the available resources are. One helpful prior element is the teacher's own understanding of the nature of texts. The word text derives from the Latin *texere* meaning 'to weave' (hence 'textiles' and 'texture'). The way forward offered by more recent knowledge gained from modern studies of discourse and genre depends upon a more flexible, sophisticated notion of what a text is than is generally evident from some traditional approaches to English.
>
> (Keith, in QCA 1999a)

The technique involves only allowing the pupils access to a very small area of the printed text at a time: possibly the first sentence, or at most the first paragraph. The readers, in groups, look in close detail at absolutely every word, and attempt to suggest not only which word classes those words might be in, but what function they are performing in the text. The teacher might ask pupils to undertake this activity with the actual book, covering up everything else not currently being studied. Alternatively, the paragraph might be photocopied (even enlarged), to enable the pupils to write any notes directly over the extract.

This might lead to the following sorts of findings, such as with the first sentence of *Holes*:

> *There is no lake at Camp Green Lake.*

The reader is already faced with a contradiction; how might that idea be important to the rest of the book? The sentence is short and direct, with nothing wasted; it is almost confrontational.

Grammar analysis: 'There' (an adverb, often used with 'is' to indicate existence) is followed by 'no' (a determiner, usually preceding a noun). The noun is 'lake', followed by the preposition 'at' (informing us where the coming noun might be in relationship to the first noun), and an extended proper noun phrase: 'Camp Green Lake'. 'Camp Green Lake' could be so evocative. 'Camp' suggests holidaying and relaxing, possibly in tents. 'Green' is a bright colour associated with life and fertility, and has the power to conjure up a verdant, rich, possibly tree lined, stretch of water when juxtaposed with 'Lake'. But there 'is no lake' at this Camp!

This sharp, direct, brisk, contradictory, slightly amusing opening has already begun to help the readers to frame an initial idea about the tone and voice of the book. A bit more information, however, would be helpful for further confirmation:

> *There once was a lake here, the largest lake in Texas.*

The reader is being sent back into the past. Not only into history for its own sake, but also to gain a sense of the huge size of the lake that once occupied the site; information we might need in the unfolding of the text. We also know more about the location of Camp Green Lake; it is in Texas, probably in the USA. The first sentence began 'There is', the second begins 'There was once'.

Grammar analysis: 'There' (an adverb, often preceding 'is' or 'was' to indicate existence) is separated from its verb 'was' by the second adverb 'once' (informing us of a former phenomenon, no longer there). 'A' is the determiner preceding the noun 'lake', but the next word is worth noting; it is 'here'. This adverb is mostly employed by speakers in the presence of their listener, to indicate something or somewhere visible to both. It would seem that the author has used it in this instance to more directly involve the reader in the narrative; as if we are listening to this narrative being recounted. The lake was not just large, it was 'the' (a determiner) 'largest' (superlative degree of an adjective) 'lake' (noun) 'in' (preposition) 'Texas' (proper noun, naming an American state).

We are suddenly, after only 19 words of the story, informed about a great deal. We have a picture of a huge lake, which has somehow disappeared. We know the setting is American, which could change the way we might feel about the word 'Camp'.

Many American children spend their summers away from their city homes, enjoying themselves in activities at 'camp'; antithetically, the Americans also invented the 'boot camp', as a device for punishing delinquent juveniles. The ambivalence and contradictions contained in the word 'camp' mirror the sense of the first sentence.

That was over a hundred years ago.

Grammar analysis: the text is still being constructed in short, direct sentences. 'That' is a pronoun, drawing together and standing in for much of the information of the previous sentence. 'Was' confirms the setting in the past, while the preposition 'over' helps to emphasise our understanding of 'more than' 'a' (determiner) 'hundred' (number/adjective) 'years' (plural noun) 'ago' (adverb indicating time).

Now it is just a dry, flat wasteland.

Grammar analysis: the final sentence in the first paragraph is again a tightly constructed, sharp statement. 'Now' (another adverb of time) pulls us directly back to the present from the past, 'it' (pronoun replacing the 'Green Lake') 'is' (present tense of verb) 'just' (adverb) indicating merely or only, as strong contrast from previous state. 'A' (determiner) 'dry' (adjective), 'flat' (adjective) 'wasteland' (the noun being described by the previous two adjectives).

The reader is, uncompromisingly, being confronted with the harshness and characterless nature of the setting, which the next few sentences will develop even more forcefully. The clearly signposted swings between the past and the present are also alerting the reader to important issues still to be pursued. The next paragraph immediately picks up that theme.

There used to be a town of Green Lake as well.

Grammar analysis: this is not a writer who offers long, detailed, rich descriptive passages. These descriptions are as clipped and barren as the settings they are establishing. 'There' (an adverb we have seen twice already in this context) is followed by 'used to be' (past tense of the verb 'to use', preceding the infinitive verb 'to be', to inform us of something that was once present) 'a' (determiner) 'town' (noun) 'of' (preposition) 'Green Lake' (proper noun, naming the town) 'as well' (adverbial phrase, meaning also). So the reader is not only wondering what happened to the lake, but is also made to consider the former town and its demise.

The town shriveled and dried up along with the lake, and the people who lived there.

Grammar analysis: 'The' (a determiner, making previous references to 'a town' more specific) 'town' (noun of the place being described) 'shriveled and dried' (past tense of two verbs, joined by the conjunction 'and', emphasising the loss of moisture and life through the repetition of two words with virtually the same meaning. One would have been sufficient, two references are indisputable. 'Along with' is a prepositional phrase, relating the drying up of the lake with the town. 'And the people who lived there' is a curious phrase; it starts with a conjunction (and) suggesting the second part of a compound sentence. We are expected, probably, to understand that the 'people' (collective noun indicating the residents of the town) grew old and the supply of them dried up, rather like the lake. But it could mean something else . . . Teachers might also refer to the American spelling of 'shriveled'.

Teachers should not be frightened about encouraging their pupils to become aware of grammar and urging them to explain how it functions in the text. As the Literacy Strategy becomes even more influential, with pupils having encountered it for some years in primary schools, so pupils will increasingly become more confident in using the grammatical terminology they have progressively acquired. It should, however, be clearly understood that the grammar is not being identified for its own sake. It is a device to begin explaining *how* the text is working. It is being used to seek patterns; to notice very obvious linguistic devices, that will in turn suggest ways of making more secure meaning in the text. There is anecdotal evidence from some primary schools, and a few secondary schools that have adopted this practice, that boys are particularly keen on grammatical analysis. They see it as a solid way of engaging with texts; as a way they can begin controlling in their own terms.

I shall not continue in the same detail with the grammatical analysis, but explore the rest of the first page in a manner suggested by the reading objectives guiding this study.

During the summer the day time temperature hovers around ninety-five degrees in the shade – if you can find any shade. There's not much shade in a big dry lake.

Pupils could be helped to notice the repetition of 'shade' three times in two sentences. They might be asked to consider 'big dry lake', without the use of a comma between the two adjectives, a normal convention.

The only trees are two old oaks on the eastern edge of the 'lake'. A hammock is stretched between the two trees, and a log cabin stands behind that.

The campers are forbidden to lie in the hammock. It belongs to the Warden. The Warden owns the shade.

In two short paragraphs of two or three sentences (again, it is worth noting that most sentences still do not exceed 16 or 17 words) the author has established the whole tone and attitude of the governing regime of the camp. 'The Warden owns the shade' is uncompromising, yet also amusing at the same time. This understanding is important. Observant readers of the cover will already be aware of the name Stanley Yelnats from the book's cover. This palindrome is very cheeky and suggests a less than serious approach to the novel. In the next 'chapter', the conclusion of Stanley's trial is described:

Stanley Yelnats was given a choice. The judge said, 'You may go to jail, or you may go to Camp Green Lake.'

Stanley was from a poor family. He had never been to camp before.

So, Stanley's inexperience and unworldliness ironically lead to him being condemned to the most gruelling of work centres, while he believes that he has chosen the 'softer option'. It is in such moments of poignancy that the novel suggests its intended attitude. We are being drawn into the narrative, and become exposed to some vivid detail and frightening moments, but the novel has also shown itself to be 'a fiction'; it is not a real event, but a very deliberate construct. We move close to it on occasions, but we also realise that we can stand apart from it and consider its constructedness.

The end of the first 'chapter' confirms this view:

Here's a good rule to remember about rattlesnakes and scorpions: If you don't bother them, they won't bother you.
Usually.
Being bitten by a scorpion or even a rattlesnake is not the worst thing that can happen to you. You won't die.
Usually.
Sometimes a camper will try to be bitten by a scorpion, or even a small rattlesnake. Then he will get to spend a day or two recovering in his tent, instead of having to dig a hole out on the lake.
But you don't want to be bitten by a yellow-spotted lizard. That's the worst thing that can happen to you. You will die a slow and painful death.
Always.

Merely looking carefully at the way the text is laid out on the page suggests that the author is structuring in a particular way. The first two sentences are followed by the one word, 'usually'; then the next section is brought to a firm conclusion with the word 'always'. There is almost a choric feel to the passage. When a writer uses these sorts of devices it is clear that we are not necessarily to accept what has been written too seriously. This is a story that will have the power to frighten, to move and to excite. It is also a novel that surprises. But it will not be one in which we are expected to believe too much.

Step 5

At this point pupils might again be asked to make predictions about the likely short term, medium term and long term developments in the novel. These predictions, written on small pieces of paper, can be kept by the teacher in separate envelopes for each pupil. They could review the questions already asked (kept in the same place) and check to see if any have yet been answered. They could raise further questions relating to matters which they want to know more about. Pupils could devise word level, sentence level or text level questions, which they then discuss.

Another way of approaching the teaching of this particular text, in line with the recommendations made on page 68, would be to study it alongside a related, complementary text. Teachers might consider also working with Gary Paulsen's *Nightjohn*. The book has one obvious positive factor: at around 80 pages it is very short. *Holes* is a novel partly concerned with education and the empowering results of education; it is about people suffering under the weight of a power they cannot resist. *Nightjohn* shares the same view of education and concerns a slave community mostly powerless to change its ways. Both books feature young people as their central characters, trapped in very challenging social circumstances over which they have little control. While *Holes* would be the 'lead' text, being given the fullest attention and even read right through, copies of *Nightjohn* could be referred to occasionally, to compare ideas, language, plot developments, or whatever was being featured as the main area of interest.

The final set of recommendations about strategies to employ in studying this text are related to the questions listed in Appendix 8.1 of the 'Reading' module in the *English Department Training 2001* manual (DfEE 2001f), distributed to all English departments. These questions are 'models' for teachers to use as ways of exploring the text level, sentence level and word level issues on which the text is constructed and its meanings made. Typical examples of text level questions are:

- what is my purpose in reading this text?
- what can I immediately begin to understand?
- before I even begin reading, what do I know and what do I expect this text will be about?
- what genre or text type am I reading?
- what sort of support might enable me to read this more independently?

(DfEE 2001f)

There are 16 more questions at this level in the Appendix.

Sentence level question examples include:

- what is immediately noticeable about the layout/presentation of this text, and what might this information indicate about the possible meaning?
- what is the average sentence length? Do the sentence lengths vary, or are they consistent? What do these facts help me to understand about the possible meanings? What effect do they create?
- are most of the sentences in statement form, or are other sentence types also used? How and why?
- does the writer break any of the expected conventions, if so to what effect?
- are there any recognisable patterns or structures in the language?

(DfEE 2001f)

There are 6 other sentence level questions offered in the manual.

Typical word level questions to ask might be:

- is the vocabulary of this text mostly familiar or are there a number of words, or sorts of words, not known?
- is the vocabulary consistent, or do changes occur at different times?
- are words used in unusual ways?
- are the words from our time or other periods?
- are puns, irony, pastiche or other forms of humour evident?

(DfEE 2001f)

Four other examples are offered.

It is essential to understand that these are *not the only questions* possible to ask of texts. I devised them, in the first instance, as a sort of 'starter kit'; modelling for teachers the types of questions appropriate in text level, sentence level and word level study contexts. English teachers (and those from other subjects) are invited to supplement these questions with others capable of bringing about similarly increased insights.

They have three main purposes. The first is to offer pupils a repertoire of possible enquiries that they can begin using independently as they grow more confident. If the definition of literacy offered on page 11 means anything to an English department, then every pupil will be supplied with such a strategic approach to new and more familiar texts, to enable strong early contact. The second is to replace the tired formulaic 'comprehension' questions some pupils are still asked to perform on texts, to demonstrate that they have read and supposedly understood what is going on in their reading. The third is to shift the intention of reading from regularly relentlessly passing through a series of texts to their conclusion, to encouraging developing readers to engage more readily with whole texts and extracts, and make sharper relations between them.

This lengthy explanation, around one text, offers an illustration of more sophisticated and different ways to teach fictional textual material. These recommendations build on the skills that pupils should have been accruing in their primary literacy hours. Even if their pupils are relatively unaware of these sorts of reading approaches by Year 7, secondary English teachers should still regard them as the recommended way of working. If young people can be prepared for the various tests they must encounter at different ages by practising these strategies, they will be in a stronger position to seek for their meanings and comment on them. Helping the pupils know the correct sorts of questions to raise about texts could be the most valuable lesson teachers can provide.

5 Rethinking Writing using the *Framework* at Key Stage 3

Writing has become, rightly, the major concern of the government agencies that monitor the curriculum, and many teachers. This anxiety should not be surprising. Writing is the most difficult literacy undertaking any one of us can tackle. Huge numbers of pupils achieving the required Levels in English at the end of Key Stages 2 and 3 often have a disparity in reading and writing attainment, with the better reading scores supporting lower attainment in writing. English teachers have long recognised that pupils entering secondary schools bring superior reading attainment, with writing skills trailing badly.

The National Literacy Strategy in primary schools insisted on a closer relationship between pupils' reading and writing experiences, with their writing programmes prescribed in a specified number of text types, based substantially on increased grammatical knowledge. This more deterministic approach has caused considerable discussion and some heated argument amongst secondary English teachers, and others interested in the development and future growth of writing. The following representations are typical of some of the heat being generated:

> For the past decade, effectively since the advent of the National Curriculum, the way that teachers have been required to approach the teaching and assessment of writing has become increasingly circumscribed within a narrowly mechanistic framework. It is bound by a paradigm which focuses on writing largely as a matter of construction and correctness – at word level, sentence level and text level. This kind of linguistic analysis is mechanistic because it pays little or no attention to the meaning of any specific piece of writing.
>
> (D'Arcy 1999)

> Changing the ways we work in order to focus on objectives: are reading and writing weaknesses at KS 3 caused solely (or mainly) by insufficient attention to grammatical rules and conventions?
>
> (Wilks 2000)

The evidence, year on year, that considerable numbers of young people, sometimes after eleven years of compulsory education, leave school unable to communicate and create confidently and reasonably accurately in English is overwhelming. As with the teaching of reading, English departments and whole-school teams have rarely established any sort of writing overview to guide the approaches and thinking they might be adopting to steer teaching and learning in writing.

The following list of 'qualities' or statements about writing, once again at a stage beyond the *Framework* objectives, could begin to offer teachers a more focused support structure. They might state that their school or department promotes a view of writing that believes:

1. a writer knows that writing is a purposeful, controlled, deliberate, text-making construct that is different from, but related to, speaking;
2. a writer knows that all writing should be designed to meet the needs of real or imagined audiences;
3. a writer knows that writing should be framed within recognisable text types or genres, and their possible combinations;
4. a writer knows that more precise and effective writing can be achieved through informed grammatical and linguistic choices;
5. a writer knows that writing can be more carefully compiled when modelled through attentive critical reading;
6. a writer knows that writing is a process, capable of continuing improvement;
7. a writer knows that writing can be used to articulate, rehearse, explore and consolidate ideas, concepts, theories, speculation and knowledge;
8. a writer knows that more successful writing can be prepared through preliminary talk;
9. a writer knows that writing skills can be improved through self-evaluation of and reflection on own progress.

These 'qualities' bear a closer examination:

1. a writer knows that writing is a purposeful, controlled, deliberate, text-making construct that is different from, but related to, speaking;
2. a writer knows that all writing should be designed to meet the needs of real or imagined audiences;
3. a writer knows that writing should be framed within recognisable text types or genres, and their possible combinations;

It is possible to find a large number of young people, having completed eleven years of compulsory education, who are unaware that in order to write successfully they must understand about a very deliberate combination of possible intellectual choices and decisions. Many inexperienced writers still think, even at 16 years of age, that writing is like 'downloading' a spoken monologue to whoever receives the material at the other end of the process, as if the audience is listening, not reading.

They can be unaware that preparing to write means:

- determining the *purpose* of the writing (is this writing intended, for instance, to describe? to explain? to argue? to amuse? to incite?);
- recognising the needs of the *audience* of the writing (do my audience know anything about this topic? will my audience be looking for a particular sort of emphasis? are my audience already familiar with my writing?);
- having a sense of the *text type* or *genre* to be tackled (e.g. 'I am attempting to construct an argument in a particular manner, using the language of persuasion).

Without those preliminary considerations, a writer will be approaching any writing task 'blind'. The 'scaffolding' resulting from these sorts of mental enquiry could offer the necessary structuring for planning and developing a piece of text. This book has already considered what a benefit an overview of textual possibilities can offer. Yet, day by day, in many classrooms, young people are asked to construct pieces of text about which they have no real knowledge, and they expend little energy wondering why it might have been necessary to write it in the first place. Writing in these circumstances is a worthless, time-consuming activity, incapable of being improved or developed. There is too little time available in school to allow this situation to continue, and teachers of all subjects should be enabled to learn sufficiently about writing to encourage its genuine growth and progress for pupils of whatever ability.

4. a writer knows that more precise and effective writing can be achieved through informed grammatical and linguistic choices;

The development of this goal should be shared by all teachers, although English staff are likely to play the biggest part. The Key Stage 3 *Framework for Teaching English* describes a 'confident writer' as one who is 'able to write for a variety of purposes and audiences, knowing the conventions and beginning to adapt and develop them' (DfEE 2001a), and offers detailed objectives in Years 7, 8 and 9 in the Sentence level columns to encourage the practice and greater understanding of this area of linguistic knowledge. The large white training folder *Literacy Across the Curriculum* (DfEE 2001e) contains an early module outlining an essential approach to *Writing non-fiction*, which should be shared intensively with all staff. Part of the module is a 17-page invaluable handout, which should be compulsory reading for all teachers, articulating the vital features of linguistic knowledge necessary to bring about more controlled writing choices. English teachers should also look equally closely at the grammatical characteristics of fiction texts, to explore possible foundations for weaker writers in their attempts to construct examples of different genres.

5. a writer knows that writing can be more carefully compiled when modelled through attentive critical reading;

Once again teachers are reminded, through this area of learning about writing, how closely reading and writing have to be linked in pupils' literacy understanding. To become capable writers, pupils have not only to be regularly familiarised with the necessary range of text types, but also brought into close, analytical proximity to them. It is not enough merely to read passages from subject-related textbooks, or to copy from the board pieces of text already structured for them by subject staff. A necessary engagement has to be provided as a learning intervention. Teachers must stop pupils at certain points, to ensure that they are able to articulate what purpose the text is fulfilling, how it has been constructed, and what might be worth remembering from it for future use in the pupils' own words.

This deliberate approach has to become even more pronounced in the secondary school, as pupils begin to be introduced to a wider range of text types. During the primary Literacy Strategy pupils will learn about, and revisit, examples of 'recount', 'non-chronological report', 'explanation', 'instruction', 'persuasion' and 'discussion' texts, with the expectation that they will become more confident at recognising their characterising features. As they proceed through Key Stage 3, pupils will also become introduced to 'analysis' and 'evaluation', among others.

6. a writer knows that writing is a process, capable of continuing improvement;

Adult writers rarely manage to construct their intended texts successfully at their first attempt. It is, then, most unlikely that school pupils will have mastered that capability. All writing should be brought about in stages, building on planning and drafting procedures. Practically, most teachers do not have time to attend to these developmental steps all the time, but if writing is to be given full and proper attention as a growing skill across the school, some moments should be set aside for exploring ways of demonstrating possible improvements for all pupils.

The learning aspirations embodied in the Literacy Strategy in Key Stages 1, 2 and 3 require pupils to spend time 'practising' what they are expected to carry forward into all areas of their school experience. At Key Stages 1 and 2, class teachers can often address the breadth of textual issues in the Literacy Hour, and possibly spend time constructing exemplar extracts. They then attempt to employ that new learning in real subject written contexts. The same process is much more difficult to plan for and track at Key Stage 3, when literacy issues might be learned in some English lessons, but not embedded in the writing taking place in other subjects taught by different teachers. In these circumstances, clear writing policies should be adopted and adhered to by all subject staff. If teachers of science, or geography, or design and technology want their pupils to improve as writers, then they will have to plan for, support and offer time to allow pupils to improve as writers.

7. a writer knows that writing can be used to articulate, rehearse, explore and consolidate ideas, concepts, theories, speculation and knowledge;

A great deal of writing in many schools is merely to prove that the teacher and the pupils were in the same place. That damning statement is to point out that some writing merely exists as a record of a classroom interaction, but it has not necessarily been shaped to enable the best articulation of the intended learning, or as a way of allowing the pupil to explore the issues under consideration. The writing 'just is'! Ask lots of pupils why they write, and their answer will be likely to suggest that they perceive writing as a necessary activity that takes place in schools, between 9.00 a.m. and 3.15 p.m., come what may, to prove that 'work' has been done. All teachers will recognise the example of the lesson when pupils might have been asked to talk together, and they then leave the room at the lesson's conclusion beaming to each other that they 'haven't had to do any work today!'

In the Key Stage 3 *Framework* schools will be expected to offer opportunities in all three years for pupils to 'imagine, explore, entertain', 'inform, explain, describe', 'persuade, argue, advise' and to 'analyse, review, comment'. There will not be sufficient time or opportunity to teach, promote, and practise the whole of this purposeful repertoire in English lessons, so some of these categories could be included in the planning of other subjects. Deciding on which categories should be allocated to particular subject areas will again depend on the strength of the school's writing policy. Only in schools where auditing of writing has been carried out, and a good sense of which departments promote which sorts of textual writing has been understood, will real understanding of this problem be achieved.

Finally, in this section, it is worth remembering that writing does not have to be the concluding act of study. There are other places in the development of research or exploration where writing can be profitably employed. Pupils should have opportunities to use writing to speculate and predict; they should be allocated time to explore the relevance of approaching a writing task in relevantly alternative ways;

they should be able to discuss methods that might not be eventually chosen as the final outcome.

8. a writer knows that more successful writing can be prepared through preliminary talk;

A literate classroom is a collaborative classroom, meaning that pupils should, as a matter of course, be expected to talk together regularly. One of the essential contexts for talk is in that preliminary time before pupils undertake a writing task. In classrooms where support mechanisms, such as 'writing partners', are a natural part of the writing approach, talk will be an integral part of any writing procedure. Too often, pupils are told to 'get out your books' and to 'get on with this writing'. The culture should be adapted to enable at least a short dialogue about such features as 'what is the purpose of this piece?', 'who are we writing for?' and 'which stylistic and grammatical features ought we to be taking notice of as we write?' Even as an absolute minimum, regular discussion of these aspects as preliminaries to any writing task could lead to evident improvement in writing in a short time in all schools.

9. a writer knows that writing skills can be improved through self-evaluation of and reflection on own progress.

The case for pupils understanding and taking greater responsibility for their own development has been clearly made elsewhere in this book. Writers, like readers and speakers and listeners – indeed, all language users – will not make real progress and want to meet new challenges unless they have an idea of what they are attempting to achieve. It should be increasingly possible to outline and clarify the sorts of particular skills that individuals ought to be improving to make discernible headway. The greater use of personal targets in assisting pupils to map out their own learning routes has to be applied to their linguistic development just as much as learning in any other context.

All lessons could be prefaced by attention being paid to specific language learning objectives, alongside the subject content to be learned. Pupils' language learning targets should be a shared responsibility for all teaching staff in the school community.

Recognising these areas of writing development, and adopting statements of the qualities of the writer in this manner, could lead to a school building a powerful and influential writing policy emphasising its commitment to enable pupils to:

- know that writing is different from speaking;
- write for a range of purposes;
- write for a range of real or imagined audiences;
- write in recognisable genres and text types;
- use models of texts that have been read to guide their own writing;
- write clearly and legibly, in accurate and appropriate English, conveying precise meaning;
- articulate why particular linguistic choices have been made in writing;
- make progress as writers;
- become increasingly reflective and evaluative about own writing progress.

If such an overview of writing priorities guided all writing tasks in the school, then English teachers and those from other subject areas would have a common format for subsequent discussion. If the senior member of staff responsible for literacy development then insisted on seeing evidence of this policy in the planning of all departments, a school should expect to see subsequent developments within a specified length of time.

Writing in English

The policy for writing outlined above should have just as much application in the work of the English department as it does for colleagues in the rest of the school. English teachers will probably want to achieve other writing learning gains beyond the outline policy, and such extras would be possible to add, without compromising the essential cohering developmental areas of the original. English teachers might also want to rewrite the sorts of statements being offered in terms that would be better understood by their pupils. If they are to be genuine evaluators of their own progress, pupils should know what they are attempting in terms they fully understand.

Some English teachers have expressed scepticism about the approaches to writing outlined in the primary Literacy Strategy and the Key Stage 3 *Framework*, in arguments explored in some detail earlier in this chapter. They are concerned that such procedures are 'mechanistic' and suppress some or all of the 'creative' instincts they see as intrinsically important in English lessons. After all, what is English for, some teaching colleagues reason, if it is not to encourage pupils' aesthetic insights and growth through making sensitive meanings of literary texts, and attempting to make texts like them in their writing? This is after all the stuff of the literary arts. These different approaches are not mutually exclusive. I do not believe that the desire to enable pupils to create genuinely imaginative and aesthetically worthwhile texts in any way diminishes the need to look closely at texts being read, as potential models for texts to be written. In fact, writers could not write unless they had already been exposed to texts in the first place, as readers. As they develop more sophisticated reading habits and skills, so they are better prepared to attempt more difficult and demanding writing tasks.

> Reading and writing are functionally differentiated aspects of one system, and of one set of processes. An exclusive concern with either overlooks essential characteristics shared by both. Most importantly, reading and writing are both activities that draw on the forms, structures and processes of language in its written mode. That makes reading and writing fundamentally different from speaking and listening.
>
> (Kress 1986)

This sense of using one textual knowledge to support and encourage another is illustrated in the following objective:

Year 7 Text level – Writing
10. make links between their reading of fiction, plays and poetry and the choices they make as writers.

(DfEE 2001a)

The following, representing a contrary view of writing, might be seen as the direct rebuttal of Kress's argument:

> Ursula Le Guin's phrases stress the autonomy of the imagination and the openness to experience that allows it to flourish: 'experience isn't something you go and *get* – it's a gift, and the only pre-requisite for receiving it, is that you be open to it'. Jill Pirrie's achievement lies in her capacity to induce such an openness in her pupils; in Edward Blishen's words 'she knows how to cause children to be eager'. This is not a technique or a skill that could be written into a National Curriculum document. It is an attitude, a faith, a capacity to make children believe in their own 'strength and courage and intelligence.' It is a matter of following Ted Hughes' advice to teachers (which Jill Pirrie quotes): 'Their words should not be "How to Write" but "How to say what you really mean" – which is part of the search for self-knowledge and, perhaps in one form or another, grace.'
>
> (Knight 1996)

This sort of expectation is simply not something that can be addressed in every school without a lot more knowledge of the writing process itself, and a language learning programme has to be much more inclusive than this approach suggests. (Significant in this argument is the reliance on rhetorical flourish; 'strength and courage and intelligence'.) To achieve the sorts of 'experience' and insights aspired to by the quoted passage is also possible (and even desirable) within the objectives-led approach now being recommended at Key Stage 3. The sort of grammar knowledge being urged through the Sentence level study contained within the *Framework* is designed not merely to dissect text, and leave it exhausted and flopping about like a fish out of water, but to breathe extra life and a new level of engagement in pupils' encounters with it. To know how effects have been made, how experience has been translated successfully into written form, how the recognition of shared moments of human understanding have been conveyed is the intention of the Strategy. It sets out to look beyond the commonplace, and illuminate areas of writing potential thought to be undeveloped currently in so many adolescent writers.

This writing programme outlined in the Key Stage 3 *Framework* is a considerable advance on those suggested in the analytical documents produced by SEAC (1992) and QCA (1999b), promoting specific grammatical constructions, without offering sufficient space and contexts for pupils to become familiar with such technical processes. The reading learning outlined in the previous chapter of this book modelled ways in which pupils can be encouraged to explore text in a more detailed fashion, clearly designed to offer pupils of all abilities ways of explaining how authors they are studying have achieved their particular effects and intended outcomes. Employing more than one text at a time for study, to gain confirmation and further insight into the significant techniques being employed to establish the recognisable features of a genre style, will also enable pupils to articulate better what they have discovered. This knowledge becomes the essential foundation for pupils attempting to express their own ways of carefully and precisely conveying what they have to share. All English teachers are familiar with the pupils from backgrounds rich in a range of narrative experiences, able to draw on their previous interactions as the material for successful and impressive writing; the same capabilities can now be more specifically offered to pupils of all linguistic backgrounds as a result of the Key Stage

3 programme, without diminishing the opportunities of the more able.

Guided writing techniques, carefully tailored for separate groups relative to their ability, and developed from the principles being taught in shared whole-class writing sessions, should be an area of development in all English departments. The intention of this methodology is to direct teaching more specifically to pupils' needs, and prevent the sort of general classroom 'patrolling' stance often adopted by teachers. Such a way of working requires different and more focused planning, to ensure that identified small learning gains are able to underpin progress in writing for all abilities.

Pupils should also be asked to be aware of the devices, the linguistic constructions and the elements of style they are drawing on from other sources and adopting in their own writing. They could be asked to share these with writing partners, at definite points in the writing process, as an on-going analysis of their work. Such 'frames' of writing are not intended to constrain the abilities of any pupils, and are likely to enhance the confidence of many. Those with already advanced writing abilities in Key Stage 3, clearly demonstrating that they are in excellent control of the material being constructed by their classmates, should be given directed challenges (not just more of the same) to explore personal and original ways of approaching the same or more complex material.

Writing at Key Stage 3 using the new *Framework* could offer opportunities for English teachers to explore more areas of writing development than they have previously anticipated or considered. Geoff Barton, writing in the *TES*, is positively bubbling over with ideas:

> The best texts are short and pithy: a snippet from a brochure or leaflet, a cutting from a *Daily Mail* editorial, the instructions on how to programme your video. Arid analysis will not work. Students have to explore the text actively. So write it for a different audience – someone who has owned a video previously, or for someone who is not even sure how to open the box. Make it more personal. Make it more impersonal. Make it chatty. Set the instructions out in a continuous prose paragraph. Change them into bullet points. Add more description. Cut all description. Make the verbs more active. Tell the whole thing using diagrams and labels.
>
> (Barton 2001)

Similar ideas can be generated, using the developing knowledge pupils should acquire about grammar and language, in fiction and non-fiction contexts. Pupils might be encouraged to write biography and/or autobiography, for example, from a particular 'stance'. Is the subject of this text an attractive or unpleasant character? Is the subject lively, active and busy, or modest, quiet and withdrawn? What would be the appropriate style to convey each set of contrasting characteristics? Which vocabulary should be considered?

Pupils could be asked to tell the same stories; one version employing rich description, metaphor and vivid language, and an alternative written in a tighter, more frugal, wholly spartan style. Even harder would be the challenge of writing up to four short versions of the same tale at different points along a continuum of vividness. Recounts could be devised with the sequences of events out of order, but written in such a way – with the careful use of connectives – that the audience is quite clear about the actual time-line. An English department meeting could quickly come up with a huge range of challenging writing tasks, designed to encourage and develop pupils' creative skills, while also paying attention to their increasing knowledge of genre and text types.

The following grammatical 'framing' devices were discovered and used by an able Year 6 class, in their lessons designed to improve writing of suspense texts:

- short, punchy sentences;
- occasional one word sentences;
- adverbs used as the first word in sentences;
- normal sentence structures changed, e.g. 'Before . . .'; 'To their surprise . . .'; 'At that moment . . .', etc.;
- facts hidden from the reader with the use of 'it', 'something';
- reactions of characters demonstrated through the verbs associated with them;
- use of questions in the text, as if to the reader;
- a range of linguistic effects, e.g. personification, metaphor, simile, etc.

The deliberate integration of these features in their writing enormously enhanced the quality of their work, while still enabling their creative skills to flourish. The work produced by the group was varied and unique to each writer. A genuine extra dimension had been added to their repertoire of ideas and approaches, leading to writing they could readily explain and adapt, given specific linguistic features to address. Such preparation and detail is an expectation of the Key Stage 3 programme.

English teachers will probably need to come to terms with expecting less writing from their pupils at times, although this changed expectation might come as a relief to teachers and pupils alike! While it is essential that pupils continue to practise sustained pieces of writing, for a number of reasons, it is not a requirement of the Strategy that all writing should be fully developed. If pupils are to learn, they should not always be practising through longer, sustained pieces. They should also be given opportunities to attempt alternative or comparative versions, stop to question and improve, and evaluate. Some of their writing could be collaborative, sharing intentions and possible directions as the writing is devised. Many pupils do not have to produce two or three sides of written material to demonstrate that they are not making progress, when a paragraph or two could lead to the same conclusion. Equally, pupils offering limited, but concentrated, pieces of work could be achieving at a level likely to lead to greater success, because it has been sufficient space in which to accomplish something small but significant. Sustained writing is required by the National Curriculum, and should not be eradicated from the English curriculum, but it could be more sparingly used for clearer, purposeful outcomes. One further benefit English teachers could also seek through this approach would be the reduced marking resulting from pupils' own self-assessment, both by individuals and reading partners or groups. A teacher's marking load could be seriously reduced by suggesting that pupils critically read the written work of others, before it is submitted to an adult. Providing the class is trained to undertake that task properly, it also contributes to better learning about writing.

6 Rethinking Speaking and Listening using the *Framework* at Key Stage 3

The Literacy Strategy introduced into Key Stages 1 and 2 in 1998 was heavily criticised because it lacked the essential elements of speaking and listening in its training and planning programmes. Literacy was viewed, in a disturbingly reductionist capacity, as being a matter of reading and writing, and valuable language learning opportunities were lost as a result. The QCA did, in time, produce an excellently supportive document *Teaching Speaking and Listening in Key Stages 1 and 2* (QCA 1999c), but the centrality of the importance of these language areas had been somewhat lost in the intervening time. Yet, of course, speaking and listening was constantly being employed in every classroom to bring about better reading study, and to establish and 'frame' writing activities.

The same mistake has not been repeated in the Key Stage 3 documentation, and, possibly for the first time in such detail, real attention has been given to listening learning and progression in the English and Literacy Across the Curriculum training folders. Separate modules have been written to encourage greater attention to both elements in all subjects of the curriculum. Objectives for Speaking and Listening, including those for drama, appear in columns for each of the three years, alongside the Text level Reading and Writing objectives. Many of those objectives are not exclusive to work in English, for example:

Year 7 Speaking
Pupils should be taught to:
1. use talk as a tool for clarifying ideas, e.g. *by articulating problems or asking pertinent questions;*
3. tailor the structure, vocabulary and delivery of a talk or presentation so that listeners can follow it;
4. give clear answers, instructions or explanations that are helpfully sequenced, linked and supported by gesture or other visual aid;
5. promote, justify or defend a point of view using supporting evidence, example and illustration which are linked back to the main argument;

(DfEE 2001a)

Teachers in all subject areas are clearly expected to pay greater attention to the potential of including speaking and listening objectives (and learning) into the planning of their work, and their teaching strategies.

Teachers should regard language learning as 'holistic', by which I mean that each area of language knowledge (reading, writing, speaking and listening) is always developed simultaneously. Pupils never just learn separately to read, or write, or speak, or listen. They are always learning something about all four language elements while engaged in linguistic activities, although particular attention might foreground one relative to the others.

Much previous speaking and listening work in English has been planned, at best, cursorily, and not always regularly designed to bring about measurable progression. Furthermore, speaking and listening is usually much more structured in English than in lessons of most other subjects! The DfEE has published a *Year 7 Speaking and Listening Bank* (DfEE 2001g) to offer greater support and assistance in the planning and progression of these two vital areas. Pupils need to build secure skills of speaking to enable more confident articulation of ideas and learning, and to bring about more focused and directed questions of their experiences. Large numbers of young people are not accustomed to listening carefully, or even really knowing what to listen out for! Culturally, listening is given less and less attention, and practised only minimally. As a society we watch much more than we listen. Yet, an enormous proportion of time in school involves pupils listening, so it is essential that pupils learn to speak and listen in different ways, for different tasks.

Speaking should be seen as more closely related to writing, even if it is only to enable the clearer distinction between them. All writing tasks would be improved by pupils sharing their expectations about, and the criteria of, the texts they are intending to create. Speaking should also be built into the reading procedures taking place in classrooms; to encourage the increased sharing of insights and meaning being discovered in textual encounters. The provision of reading, writing, and speaking and listening objectives, alongside each other on the same page in the *Framework* document, offers the clearest message about integrating them in units of language learning, as illustrated in the exemplar module in the next chapter.

As with the teaching and understanding of reading and writing, schools should also emphasise their commitment to speaking and listening development by cohering their approaches through shared policy. They might state, for example, that their school/department believes that:

1. pupils know that speakers can take increasingly purposeful control of talk in a range of contexts;
2. pupils know that effective speaking meets the needs of particular audiences and contexts;
3. pupils know that listening skills can be improved by attending to particular events in more focused ways;
4. pupils know that reading and writing attainment can be supported and improved through talking about and listening to the ways meanings are sought and constructed in texts;
5. pupils know that learning can be improved through exploring opportunities to articulate what is being studied in their own words;
6. pupils know that speaking and listening attainment can be improved through evaluating and reflecting on what is being said, and how well listening has been used.

In turn, these statements would allow a school to publish a policy that describes its aims to enable pupils:

- to communicate effectively by speaking with increasing confidence, clarity and fluency, and listening with increasing care and attention;
- to speak appropriately in a variety of settings, for a range of audiences;
- to develop a wide range of speaking skills on increasingly more complex subjects in more demanding contexts;
- to think carefully and organise thinking before speaking;
- to listen attentively to increasingly challenging discourses;
- to respond sensitively and reflectively to what has been heard;
- to evaluate and reflect on their talking and listening abilities, as a way of improving those skills.

While a school could build a better 'talking and listening culture' if teachers in all subjects were aware of, and incorporated in their lessons, the speaking and listening objectives in the *Framework* folder, English (and possibly drama) teachers will be more likely to address the 'Drama' objectives at the bottom of the column in each year. These separate, but related, objectives offer a range of opportunities for English staff to provide a range of role-play situations. Pupils do not have to be in the drama studio, the school hall, or behind the stage to conduct drama-based activities in which they can explore and rehearse 'real' language contexts. The English classroom, with possibly pairs of pupils working together at their desks, can be just as suitable. In an English programme intended to be: 'highly interactive', 'active and purposeful', 'varied in style and distinguished by a fast pace and strong focus', and 'secured in use and meaningful in context', these particular objectives can contribute enormously.

7 Planning for English in Key Stage 3: integrating the *Framework* objectives

General planning considerations

The introduction of the Key Stage 3 English strand could be an important, but burdensome, time for an English department, as it gives a rare opportunity for the English team to reconsider and possibly change planning procedures to outline more focused learning intentions. A department will of course make what modifications it deems necessary, depending on how effectively it currently sets about planning. The NLS directors responsible for the Key Stage 3 programme claim that they do not want teachers to rewrite all their planning documentation:

> Many schools will wish to adapt their existing format, bearing in mind the requirements . . . Although the Framework implies new emphases, it is expected that much of the existing Schemes of Work will be easily adapted. Most important is the need to organise teaching around specific objectives in the Framework; simply touching on them is not enough. Therefore, the job of measuring up existing Schemes of Work to the Framework is more than a tick-list activity: it is a matter of re-orientating what is done, rather than adding in extra topics.
>
> (DfEE 2001a: 19)

Yet, any existing Schemes of Work that can simply be updated by having a few clear objectives added, but otherwise continue to be taught, virtually untouched, will be rare. More likely, many English departments will have to make substantial changes to the present documentation articulating their teaching overview, which is why it should not be a rushed and hasty exercise. From September 2001 it could, realistically, take anything up to two years or so for a department to settle into a satisfactory pattern of planning with which it will become comfortable, and choose to adopt in the future.

The *Framework* document regularly stresses that a significant change to be achieved in English through the Strategy is the emphasis on learning:

i The Key Stage 3 National Strategy promotes **learning** that is:
- active and highly-motivated;
- purposeful;
- creative and imaginative; etc. (DfEE 2001a: 16)

ii The implications of this for lesson organisation are few, but very significant:
- more explicit teaching, with attention to Word and Sentence level skills;
- an emphasis on learning rather than just completing coursework or getting through set texts; etc. (p. 17)

iii The National Literacy Strategy has already developed ways of working more effectively in these ways, through the use of . . .
- plenaries to consolidate the learning objectives; etc. (p. 17)

But the objectives themselves, as set out in the *Framework*, are *not* learning objectives. They are written as separate activities, stating the sorts of coverage of the English/language curriculum expected to be made by all classes during the course of the school year. They all begin with verbs such as: 'appraise', 'review', 'answer', 'identify', 'promote', 'make links', which are things to do. Of course, it is possible to learn how to 'recognise how print, sounds and still or moving images combine to create meaning', by becoming more accomplished in the practice of seeking meaning in those texts, but the objectives – sound as most of them are – do not exist in isolation. To bring about the worthwhile long-term *learning* from which the pupils will benefit as developing language users, the English department has to combine these separate objectives and then shape them into broad, overview learning intentions. These intentions should be carefully considered and constructed only after the department has agreed a number of important background details.

How the objectives will be combined and focused will depend on views about the sorts of readers, writers, speakers and listeners the department believes it is attempting to promote and realise. Models of this sort of discussion are given in Chapters 4, 5 and 6 of this book, and they should be seen in the context of language/literacy development in the whole curriculum, as argued in the second chapter.

Long-term planning

The next step is to have a clear long-term sense of what the English curriculum will contain across Key Stages 3 *and* 4. Both Key Stages should be considered, because one of the roles of Key Stage 3 must be seen as preparation for the next step of a pupil's linguistic and literacy development. Another reason for establishing a clear picture of the five years of secondary compulsory education is that the National Curriculum English Orders set out the statutory textual coverage over two Key Stages, without any sort of suggestion at which point of the course any one of them should be taught. So, as the *Framework* reminds teachers:

> The National Curriculum for English prescribes the range of literature to be studied over Key Stages 3 and 4:
> - two Shakespeare plays
> - drama by major playwrights
> - two pre-1914 fiction texts
> - two post-1914 fiction texts
> - four pre-1914 poets
> - four post-1914 poets
> - recent and contemporary works
> - writers from different cultures and traditions
> - literary non-fiction
> - information and reference texts
> - media and moving image texts
>
> (DfEE 2001a: 14)

(This list would actually make a marvellous resource for textual study in its own right. Ask a sharp Year 10 or 11 group what they think this list is, who devised it, what it represents, and whether the order of texts tells us anything. They could suggest what questions are raised by some of the terms used.)

> *The Framework for teaching English* is based closely on the Programmes of Study for English in the revised National Curriculum of 2000. Framework objectives for Years 7, 8 and 9 provide a framework for progression and full coverage of the English Order.

> (DfEE 2001a: 9)

The textual contents of the National Curriculum are not the only feature of the English Orders to be related to the Framework objectives. The requirements for certain sorts of study have been woven into the objectives as well. By way of example, it is possible to see the following requirements in the 'Drama' subsection of the 'En 1 Speaking and Listening' Programme of Study:

> Drama
> 4. To participate in a range of drama activities and to evaluate their own and others' contributions, pupils should be taught to:
> (a) use a variety of dramatic techniques to explore ideas, issues, text, and meanings
> (b) use different ways to convey action, character, atmosphere and tension when they are scripting and performing in plays (for example, through dialogue, movement, pace)
> (c) appreciate how the structure and organisation of scenes and plays contribute to dramatic effect
> (d) evaluate critically performances of drama that they have watched or in which they have taken part.

> (DfEE/QCA 1999)

These areas of curriculum coverage are then mirrored in the Framework objectives below, and continue through the objectives in Years 8 and 9.

> Year 7 Speaking and Listening
> Drama
> 15. develop drama techniques to explore in role a variety of situations and texts or respond to stimuli;
> 16. work collaboratively to devise and present scripted and unscripted pieces, which maintain the attention of the audience;
> 17. extend their spoken repertoire by experimenting with language in different roles and dramatic contexts . . .
> 19. reflect on and evaluate their own presentations and those of others.

> (DfEE 2001a: 25)

The other important reason for establishing a long-term view of planning is also made clear in the *Framework:* departments will want to track progression in textual experiences and the learning made possible from them over the whole duration of a pupil's experiences with the English team: 'For example, pupils may encounter scenes by Shakespeare in primary school, or in Year 7, before studying a whole play in Year 8 or 9' (DfEE 2001c).

So, effective long-term planning will have ensured that an English team has:

- established a clear overview of the subject;
- described a sense of continuity from Key Stage 2 to the end of Key Stage 4;
- articulated a view of the sorts of textual engagements thought necessary to provide worthwhile learning;
- included in their studies all the texts required by the National Curriculum;
- established a broad and balanced programme of studies;
- related similar areas of study, and identified helpful contrasting potential textual insights, to stimulate greater interest and learning;
- related issues of word level, sentence level and text level study, to promote clearer language learning;
- ensured a balanced coverage of reading, writing, speaking and listening objectives;
- established a realistic and challenging pace for textual and language study;
- anticipated a supportive and properly formative assessment structure;
- prepared pupils appropriately for examinations and tests.

In reality English departments have rather less flexibility about some of these matters than might previously have been suggested. For instance, the current Key Stage 3 testing requirements make it essential that all Year 9 pupils study a Shakespeare play, to prepare them properly for the end of Key Stage test. The GCSE syllabus will also dictate certain sorts of textual study for the same reasons. These imperatives, imposed externally, also make a strong argument for having an up-to-date, flexible overview, to assure the team that all necessary demands have been addressed.

Medium-term planning

Medium-term planning would normally provide a picture of the work taking place in single units of related study, comprising a series of lessons lasting from two or three weeks up to a half term. The plan names the area of study and possibly even points in its title to the learning overview (or 'learning big idea' as we describe it in Milton Keynes) expected as the assessable outcome of the unit. It will suggest how many lessons the unit should take and will also state the sets, or groups, for whom it has been designed.

The medium-term plan will be the stage when, having decided the focus of the unit, the English teachers survey the available objectives designed to promote further insights in that area of study, and combine those likeliest to bring about the *learning purpose(s)* of the module. English teachers *should be quite prepared to add other related and supportive objectives not listed in the Framework*, if they feel that their contribution will ensure even better learning. While the Framework objectives are a helpful, strongly recommended (and mostly reasonable) starting point, they are not the only approaches to the textual, linguistic and meaning-making considerations of many English lessons. This is yet another area where the professional decision-making of the teacher is not being constrained, or 'straitjacketed', as the detractors of the Strategy often represent what they regard as the 'de-skilling' results of this initiative. Concentrating on the large range of objectives offered in the *Framework* will enable subject staff to track more carefully the different sorts of areas of study (called 'name tags' in pages 42–5 of the *Framework*).

Name of unit: 'To learn how writers deal with difficult, emotional and feeling issues, by reading examples of published texts and by pupils creating written examples of their own.'

Time: 5 weeks (3 hours of English each week)

To be studied by: mixed ability Year 8 class

Main resource: *Dear Nobody* by Berlie Doherty

Support resources: *Face* by Benjamin Zephaniah/*The Snake-stone* by Berlie Doherty/*Tasting the Thunder* by Gary Paulsen/more able readers possibly introduced to *Postcards from No-man's Land* by Aidan Chambers

Text level objectives:
Reading:
  4. review their developing skills as active, critical readers who search for meaning using a range of reading strategies;
  5. trace the development of themes, values or ideas in texts;
  7. identify the ways implied and explicit meanings are conveyed in different texts; e.g. *irony, satire;*
  10. analyse the overall structure of a text to identify how key ideas are developed, e.g. *through the organisation of the content and the patterns of language used;*
  16. recognise how texts refer to and reflect the culture in which they were produced, e.g. *in their evocation of place and values.*

Writing:
  5. develop the use of commentary and description in narrative, e.g. *by addressing the reader directly;*
  6. experiment with figurative language in conveying a sense of character and setting;
  7. experiment with different language choices to imply meaning and to establish the tone of a piece, e.g. *ironic, indignant;*

Speaking and Listening:
  2. tell a story, recount an experience or develop an idea, choosing and changing the mood, tone, and pace of delivery for particular effect;
  10. use talk to question, hypothesise, speculate, evaluate, solve problems and develop thinking about complex issues and ideas;
  13. recognise and build on other people's contributions;
  15. (drama) explore and develop ideas, issues, and relationships through work in role;

Figure 7.1 Suggested planning approach

Teaching sequence: (all lessons to begin with a 10-minute starter session, planned separately)

Week 1

- read and study intensively the first section through close reading methods (see Chapter 4), identifying vocabulary/structure/style/voices;
- discuss (fictional) difficult issues (role play?) involving people's emotions/people being moved;
- all pupils to be supported in reading first 37 pages in class (guided reading);
- able pupils (and other volunteers) to read on;
- most able pupils – make selection from other text list for personal reading.

Week 2

- read to page 75 (one intensive session to confirm features discovered in first week);
- for homeworks, pupils make comparisons between extracts from other texts (for least able readers)/from whole texts (for average and more able readers);
- in groups, role play and develop thinking about difficult/feeling issues;
- explore character through talk;
- introduce writing topic (personal writing about difficult emotional situation) using effects suggested on writing objectives.

Week 3

- read to page 116 (some shared reading);
- pupils read alternative extracts/whole texts and discuss related, similar effects;
- guided writing: demonstration of writing on difficult issue/first person feelings piece; drafting pupils' own writing (some guided writing);
- for homeworks, pupils draft moving/difficult emotional piece, for reading by response writing partners.

Week 4

- read to page 164 (some guided reading);
- discuss, predict and compare possible endings;
- guided writing: review drafts, comparing pieces in writing groups (differentiated length and criteria);
- longer plenary (15 minutes) third lesson, to allow pupils to share reflections on success of own and others' writing;
- for homeworks, pupils read/continue writing from class discussion.

Week 5

- read to end;
- guided writing to support completed writing;
- discussion about actual ending/looking back through text to find clues;
- final longer plenary to share evaluations of selected pupils.

Figure 7.1 continued

It is at the medium-term planning stage that the most effective identification of the learning overview (or 'big idea') can be made. Approaching the unit, the teachers ought to ask some straightforward, tough questions, the answers to which will give guidance about the possible objectives to choose:

- Why are we choosing this unit? (Answers might have to do with National Curriculum coverage/identified needs/ensuring progression as readers, writers, and speakers and listeners according to the departmental beliefs/essential features of a proper English curriculum, as agreed by the department, etc.)
- Does this unit offer substantial learning opportunities?
- In which ways will our pupils improve as readers, writers, speakers and listeners (generally, as language users) as a result of having studied this unit?
- What are the absolutely 'bottom line' learning indicators we would expect all our pupils to be able to demonstrate after completing this unit?
- What other, staged, skills or abilities would we expect some pupils to be able to demonstrate, with support?
- Which objectives would contribute to these agreed outcomes?
- Which would be the most appropriate, helpful and realistically challenging resources we could use to study and support in this module?

Figure 7.1 offers an example of the way a department might approach this planning task.

Some of the preliminary departmental discussion could have included the following topics, based on the suggested list of questions which follow.

Why are we choosing this unit? Dear Nobody is an excellent 'recent and contemporary work', satisfying a National Curriculum requirement; it offers a fine opportunity for integrating reading, writing, speaking and listening objectives; it deals with sensitive issues in a convincing manner, able to engage and motivate boys, as well as girls; it is written in a powerful, first person manner, offering robust modelling for pupils' own writing; the book's content and style offers worthwhile contrasts with other books on related topics.

Does this unit make substantial learning opportunities possible? Yes, through the combination of reading, writing, and speaking and listening objectives; pupils can learn much about a delicate, sensitive writing style; they can learn about sharing difficult narratives; they can learn how to construct difficult, sensitive pieces of narrative or commentary; they can learn to listen to each other, as they attempt to discuss and act out challenging role-play situations.

In which ways will our pupils improve as readers, writers, speakers and listeners as a result of having studied this unit? Relative to the 'qualities of the reader'/'qualities of the writer' criteria, the pupils should learn:

- to activate a growing repertoire of questions in engagements with new and unfamiliar texts;
- to become better predictors of the ways texts work and have a better knowledge of genre;

- to write for particular purposes;
- to use writing as a way of expressing emotions in clear ways;
- to write for an identified audience;

and speaking and listening capabilities should be improved in respect of:

- pupils' skills of role play and listening with understanding.

It should be clear that this unit is already one that can be seen to offer substantial learning potential. It employs some powerful texts, and makes good relations between them. The reading, writing, and speaking and listening activities are closely connected, and support identifiable short-term learning objectives, capable of being independently monitored and contributing to the overall 'learning big idea'.

Medium-term planning will, then, in conclusion:

- shape an overview of each unit or module of study included in the long-term plan;
- provide an outline to guide the team of teachers working with each year group in the school;
- ensure a balanced of word level, sentence level and text level study within each unit;
- articulate broad learning aims;
- make decisions about actual texts, or types of texts, and other resources required to support the unit or module;
- ensure a balance and clear relationship of reading, writing, speaking and listening objectives and activities;
- establish expectations about the pace of the lessons in the unit or module.

Short-term planning

When a department has decided what the curriculum overview will comprise, what the learning objectives the pupils should cover will be, and what the broad learning overview will look like, then the individual teachers should have a chance to decide how they will frame and shape their unique lessons to incorporate all those agreed features. And they should, at the same time, decide the nature of the resources they will most appropriately employ to support and assist those objectives. The short-term plan is the actual set of notes intended to guide and remind each teacher, week by week and day by day, how to engage their pupils; the main points to emphasise in each lesson; which activities to set up and such details as which group will be supported in guided reading or writing.

The short-term plan should:

- outline the particular activities students should encounter to achieve the learning intentions;
- pin down the short-term learning gains which are intended to contribute to the overall broader improvement of reading, writing, speaking and listening skills and attainment;
- specify the sorts of questions, prompts and supporting dialogue to be employed in shared and guided reading and writing;

- determine layers or approaches to enable differentiation;
- specify the pages/extracts of the particular texts being employed for reading, or the criteria for writing tasks, or speaking and listening activities;
- set out the assessment opportunities to be pursued;
- describe the stages of learning for teachers and students;
- outline the issues to be explored in the plenary session;
- act as a general aide-mémoire for teachers.

In the past, the short-term plan has often been thought of as the most important part of the teaching and learning process. But it can only be really effective in those instances where the medium-term plan has already substantially articulated what the learning overview will be for *all* pupils. Each individual member of staff, making up the Year team, will then know of those vital features to be addressed in their separate classrooms, to ensure that, whatever the shape and structure of the lesson, or possibly the different resources being used, the learning outcomes should be as close as possible for all.

Good short-term plans will also be sensitive to assessment. Teachers using such plans will have some space available to record how well the whole class, or certain groups, or even individual children have learned and understood what has been intended, or even to note surprises not originally planned for. (English lessons are like that!) This information can then lead to adaptations being required in subsequent planning, or, sometimes, where learning has been slight or disappointing, the necessary reworking of the original material to bring about greater eventual success.

Short-term planning should also be one of the means by which a Head of English or Key Stage Manager can monitor the work of members of the department. It is a device by which the member of staff with overall responsibility can judge whether the agreed programme for any year group has been consistently applied to all groups. It should be able to give a sense of the shape and pace of lessons, and the suitability of resources, as well as the level of challenge being expected.

Within the last three months I have held a conversation with English teachers who informed me that they 'did their own thing' in their Key Stage 3 lessons. Twelve years after the introduction of the National Curriculum, and its attendant Programmes of Study, outlining a broad entitlement curriculum, this situation should no longer be possible. English teachers should always have a clear idea of what they are intending to teach, and more importantly, what they want their pupils to learn. The learning might not always be as precise and accurate as described in the planning, because language and linguistic gains do not always come about in that easily fashioned manner, but they should bear some passing resemblance to the original intentions. If there is too large a discrepancy between what was stated as the learning intention and what actually transpires, then the aim might need to be stated with greater precision or clarity. If a class learns a lot more than was intended, then members of staff should congratulate themselves and try to analyse how they achieved such a remarkable result, so they can use those methods again!

8 Additional guidance on inclusion

The Strategy is meant to be truly and wholly inclusive.

The final 15-page section of the *Framework for Teaching English* (DfEE 2001a) is liable to be overlooked unless teachers have specific reasons to search there. Yet, it makes clear that all pupils, unless excused from the National Curriculum because of some disabling condition, are expected to be included in the teaching and learning programme provided by the Key Stage 3 Strategy. They are also expected to make progress as language users through the support it is capable of supplying.

In mainstream schools with a proportion of pupils with special needs, the SENCO or Head of Special Needs will need to work closely with the Head of English. It is essential that both teachers share a view of language and literacy learning and development, to ensure that the support being offered, either through pupil withdrawal or learning assistants working alongside pupils in lessons, coheres. Once more, this collaborative context places greater emphasis on whole-school principles and policies guiding English, language and literacy growth.

Three principles in relation to inclusion are established in the National Curriculum documentation and have just as much significance with the Key Stage 3 English and Literacy Across the Curriculum strands:

1. setting suitable learning challenges (recognising what pupils' learning needs might be and setting work with high expectations);
2. responding to pupils' diverse learning needs (securing opportunities to achieve and recognising different interests, experiences and strengths which influence learning);
3. overcoming potential barriers to learning and assessment for individuals and groups of pupils.

This last principle is described in three broad groups:

Pupils with Special Educational Needs (SEN);
Pupils with disabilities;
Pupils who are learning English as an Additional Language (EAL).

Pupils with Special Educational Needs (SEN)

The *Framework* recognises and makes recommendations for pupils with different degrees of special needs:

1. Those working just below national age-related expectations: pupils arriving in Key Stage 3 with a Level 3 in English might be capable, with the right sort of support and extra attention, to achieve after only a short time, at Level 4. These pupils should be assessed against the criteria offered in the individual Progress Units: Writing Organisation; Information Retrieval; Spelling; Reading Between the Lines; Phonics and Sentences. Those pupils who will benefit from these intensive structures should be allocated to them as soon as possible.

2. Pupils who are out of step, i.e. working well below national expectations for their age group, may have a huge range of different barriers to learning, but will probably be working at Levels 1 and 2. Vitally, the *Framework* document states explicitly: 'pupils working at level 1 and 2 are entitled to a rich and full curriculum. Literacy should liberate them in the other subjects, and not deny them access' (DfEE 2001a). Ways of supporting children in this group might include:

   - 'casting back' to find suitable, relevant objectives in the primary literacy *Framework* (DfEE 1998); e.g. not pursuing spelling objectives, but drawing on phonics work from Key Stages 1 or 2;
   - support from learning support assistants, working under close direction from the teacher, to ensure that the central elements of the lesson are better understood and 'translated' into terms the pupil can comprehend;
   - undertaking some further consolidation of background material, when the rest of the class is dealing with independent learning tasks;
   - the pupil possibly enjoying some extra time beyond the English lessons, but *not* withdrawn from them!

3. Pupils working significantly below age-related expectations: most pupils in this group are in special schools, but a few will be on the roll in mainstream secondary schools. Many special schools have been used to adapting the primary *Framework* to meet the needs of such pupils since the implementation of the Strategy in 1998. They have worked around the issues to be found in substantial texts, some even studying extracts or simplified versions of Shakespeare! The teachers choose objectives selectively, attempting to meet the short-term needs of pupils, intended to bring about immediate learning gains, as stepping stones to further development. While the word and sentence level objectives, and those relating to reading and writing will mostly be taken from the primary *Framework*, teachers should be able to find appropriate speaking and listening objectives from the Key Stage 3 publication.

   Often the work is carried out for 15 to 20 minutes at a time, in recognition that sixty continuous minutes is too demanding. Sometimes teachers, parents and governors have provided 'story sacks' (supporting reading resources, including 'props' to make the events in books more vivid and real) and other lively materials to enable pupils to engage more closely with the narratives being studied.

   Pupils with particular communication difficulties, such as those with autistic spectrum disorders, require well-structured, stage-by-stage lessons. They will respond better to very explicit, direct and well-focused learning aims, but these can be devised from the objectives of the Key Stage 3 English programme, although progress will be necessarily much slower.

4. Pupils with emotional and behavioural difficulties: sometimes such pupils have

behavioural difficulties because their limited literacy capabilities have prevented them from making progress in mainstream lessons in the past. These pupils could benefit greatly from taking part in more structured, purposeful, objective-led lessons, with a range of activities allowing for changes within the space of each lesson. It is essential that these pupils are given appropriate and challenging tasks; their boredom and its consequent disruptive behaviour will only be exacerbated by work at too low a level.

Planning work capable of yielding short-term gains and lots of 'mini-successes' could lead to much greater achievement. Emphasis on pupil–teacher/pupil–pupil interactivity, and exploratory exercises, will enable these pupils to take a fuller part in their own learning.

A general principle to be acknowledged by all staff dealing with special needs pupils is to avoid withdrawal whenever possible. Pupils should be learning alongside their peers if they can; to be withdrawn from English/literacy lessons to have extra literacy support is perverse!

Pupils who are learning English as an Additional Language (EAL)

The National Literacy Strategy in primary schools has demonstrated that EAL pupils, even those unable to speak much English, can benefit enormously from whole-class participation, where their particular needs are also being addressed. They need to hear properly modelled instances of structured teacher talk; they need to have opportunities for making clear links between spoken and written texts, and they need to see texts at work in real situations and contexts.

It is essential that EAL learners have their earlier learning experiences, in both their home-language literacy and English literacy, taken fully into account when plans are being devised for them. The Key Stage 3 *Framework* makes a number of very clear recommendations that are essential in the guidance of English teachers and colleagues in other subjects. Yet again, shared policy and approaches to language learning are essential for genuine progression by pupils qualifying for this attention.

Supporting and challenging gifted and talented pupils

Some criticism has been justifiably made about the lack of challenge for more able language users in the Primary Literacy Strategy. Teachers in Key Stages 1 and 2, who have worked hard to come to terms with the demands of the Strategy, improving the English/literacy skills of their mainstream pupils, have given insufficient attention – so the argument goes – to those who were already linguistically confident and successful. It is a matter still requiring more attention in primary classrooms.

The Key Stage 3 English programme should be seen as quite capable of providing a challenging and appropriately demanding programme of study for the more able pupils, *as long as the school or department has a clear view about the more able, and related guiding policy, in the first place*. The objectives describe an overview of learning requirements for all; individual teachers then have the power to make those objectives as interconnected, taxing and tough as they think necessary. Some of the recommendations about studying complementary and comparative texts earlier in this book would offer an opportunity for further and wider study. The textual knowledge writing demands of this programme make possible any number of ways of structuring writing tasks to ensure that more able writers are paying constant attention to broadening their writing repertoires. The more able can be expected to undertake preparation for lessons, and closer language exploration between lessons.

Most importantly, teachers of English should not merely add 'extension' activities to the normal demands of any mainstream class, as the usual way of dealing with the more able. This is often what happens in classrooms where the able pupils have finished their tasks earlier than their mainstream peers. To be able to develop fully the capabilities of the more able it is necessary to plan discrete, properly focused activities *at the level of these pupils* from the outset, and not to cobble together a few extra stages of work at a lower level.

The last four pages of the *Framework* offer detailed guidance and recommendations for thinking more specifically about appropriate planning for these pupils. The Key Stage 3 English programme should, in no circumstances, constrain what pupils are capable of learning in the subject. It will only be working in a worthwhile and successful manner if it enhances the linguistic, literacy and meaning-making capabilities of all young people.

References

Adams, M. (1990) *Beginning to Read.* Cambridge, Mass.: MIT Press.

Barton, G. (1999) 'The state we're in'. Book review in the *Times Educational Supplement*, 22 January, p. 24.

Barton, G. (2001) 'Unexpected genres'. *TES Curriculum Special: English*, 9 February, pp. 6, 7.

Beard, R. (1998) *National Literacy Strategy: Review of Research and Other Related Evidence.* London: DfEE.

Cairney, T. (1995) *Pathways to Literacy.* London: Cassell.

Carter, R. (1988) 'Some pawns for Kingman: Language education and English teaching', in *Applied Linguistics in Society.* Papers from the Twentieth Anniversary Meeting of the British Society for Applied Linguistics, September 1987.

Crystal, D. (1995) *The Cambridge Encyclopaedia of the English Language.* Cambridge: Cambridge University Press.

D'Arcy, P. (1999) *Two Contrasting Paradigms for the Teaching and the Assessment of Writing.* Sheffield: NAAE, NAPE & NATE.

Davies, C. (1996) *What Is English Teaching?* Buckingham: Open University Press.

Daw, P. (1995) 'Differentiation and its meanings' in *English and Media* magazine, No. 32, summer, pp. 11–15.

Dean, C. and Henry, J. (2001) 'Spelling lists scorned as "control freakery"'. *Times Educational Supplement*, 27 April, p. 3.

Dean, G. (2000) *Teaching Reading in Secondary Schools.* London: David Fulton Publishers.

Dean, R. (1978) *The Induction of Autophagy in Isolated Insect Fat Body by β-Ecdysone.* London: Pergamon Press.

Derewianka, B. (1990) *Exploring How Texts Work.* NSW, Australia: PETA.

DES (Department of Education and Science) (1975) *A Language for Life.* Report of the Committee of Inquiry under the Chairmanship of Sir Alan Bullock FBA. London: HMSO.

DES (1988) *Report of the Committee of Inquiry into the Teaching of English Language.* London: HMSO.

DfEE ((Literacy Task Force) (1997) *The Implementation of the National Literacy Strategy.* London: DfEE.

DfEE (1998) *The National Literacy Strategy: Framework for Teaching.* London: DfEE.

DfEE (1999a) *The National Literacy Strategy: Key Stage Literacy Conferences (LEA File).* London: DfEE.

DfEE (1999b) *The National Literacy Strategy: Spelling Bank: Lists of Words and Activities for the Key Stage 2 Spelling Objectives.* London: DfEE.

DfEE (2000) *The National Literacy Strategy: Grammar for Writing.* London: DfEE.

DfEE (Standards and Effectiveness Unit) (2001a) *Key Stage 3 National Strategy: Framework for Teaching English: Years 7, 8 and 9.* London: DfEE.

DfEE (2001b) *Key Stage 3 National Strategy: Management Guide: Lessons from the Pilot.* London: DfEE.

DfEE (2001c) *Year 7 Spelling Bank*. London: DfEE.

DfEE (2001d) *Year 7 Sentence Level Bank*. London: DfEE.

DfEE (2001e) *Literacy Across the Curriculum* (training folder). London: DfEE.

DfEE (2001f) *English Department Training 2001*. London: DfEE.

DfEE (2001g) *Year 7 Speaking and Listening Bank*. London: DfEE.

DfEE (2001h) *Year 7 Progress Unit – Spelling*. London: DfEE.

DfEE/QCA (Qualifications and Curriculum Authority) (1999) *The National Curriculum: Key Stages 3 and 4*. London: DfEE/QCA.

Halliday, M. and Hasan, R. (1989) *Language, Context and Text: Aspects of Language in a Social-Semiotic Perspective*. Oxford: Oxford University Press.

Hay McBer (2000) Research into Teacher Effectiveness Report to the Department for Education and Employment. London: DfEE.

Inglis, F. (1969) *The Englishness of English Teaching*. London: Ginn.

Keith, G. (1997) 'Teach Yourself English Grammar', *English and Media* magazine, No. 36, summer.

Knight, R. (1996) *Valuing English*. London: David Fulton Publishers.

Kress, G. (1986) 'Interrelations of reading and writing', in Wilkinson, A. (ed.) *The Writing of Writing*. Milton Keynes: Open University Press.

Kress, G. (1989) *Linguistic Processes in Sociocultural Practice*. Oxford: Oxford University Press.

Littlefair, A. (1991) *Reading All Types of Writing*. Milton Keynes: Open University Press.

Littlefair, A. (1992) 'Reading and writing across the curriculum', in Harrison, C. and Coles, M. (eds) (1992) *The Reading for Real Handbook*. London: Routledge.

MacDonald, I. (2001) 'A strategy too far?' *Times Educational Supplement*, 25 May, p. 8.

Ofsted (Office for Standards in Education) (2000) *The Annual Report of Her Majesty's Chief Inspector of Schools 1998/99*. London: The Stationery Office.

Perera, K. (1984) *Children's Writing and Reading – Analysing Classroom Language*. Oxford: Blackwell.

Poulson, L. (1998) *The English Curriculum in Schools*. London: Cassell.

QCA (Qualifications and Curriculum Authority) (1999a) *Not Whether But How: Teaching Grammar in English at Key Stages 3 and 4*. London: QCA.

QCA (1999b) *Improving Writing at Key Stages 3 and 4*. London: QCA.

QCA (1999c) *Teaching Speaking and Listening in Key Stages 1 and 2*. London: QCA.

SEAC (School Examinations and Assessment Council) (1992) *Key Stage 3 Pupils' Work Assessed: English*. London: SEAC.

Stoll, L. and Fink, D. (1996) *Changing our Schools: Linking School Effectiveness and School Improvement*. Buckingham: Open University Press.

Udvari-Solner, A. (1996) 'Theoretical influences on the establishment of inclusive practices'. *Cambridge Journal of Education* **26**(10), pp. 101–20.

Vygotsky, L. (1986) *Thought and Language*. Cambridge, Mass.: MIT Press.

Wilkinson, A. (ed.) (1986) *The Writing of Writing*. Milton Keynes: Open University Press.

Wilks, J. (2000) 'Key Stage 3 pilot out of control'. *NATE News*, 9 September, p. 1.

Classroom texts referred to in the text

Dear Nobody (Berlie Doherty) Lions Tracks 1991

Face (Benjamin Zephaniah) Bloomsbury 1999

Holes (Louis Sacher) Bloomsbury 2000; Collins 2001

Nightjohn (Gary Paulsen) Pan 1993

Postcards from No-man's Land (Aidan Chambers) 1999

Tasting the Thunder (Gary Paulsen) Pan 1996

The Snake-stone (Berlie Doherty) Collins 1995

Index